S0-AJZ-656

HUMILITY

HUMILITY

ANDREW MURRAY

Bridge-Logos

Orlando, FL 32822 USA

Bridge-Logos
Orlando, FL 32822 USA

Humility
by Andrew Murray

Copyright © 2000 by Bridge-Logos
Reprinted 2000, 2004, 2006

All rights reserved. Under International Copyright Law, no part of this publication may be reproduced, stored, or transmitted by any means— electronic, mechanical, photographic (photocopy), recording, or otherwise—without written permission from the Publisher.

Printed in the United States of America.

Library of Congress Catalog Card Number: 2006925622
International Standard Book Number: 0-88270-854-6

Scripture quotations are from the *King James Version* of the Bible.

G481.319.BMT.m606.35250

Contents

One day I was talking with a missionary and he said to me, "Brother, remember that when God puts a desire into your heart, He will fulfill it."

That helped me; I thought of it a hundred times. I want to say the same to you who are plunging about and struggling in the quagmire of helplessness and doubt. The desire that God puts into your heart, He will fulfill.

If any are saying that God has no place for them, let them trust God and wait, and He will help them and show them their place. I have learnt to place myself before God every day, as a vessel to be filled with His Holy Spirit. He has filled me with the blessed assurance that He, as the everlasting God, has guaranteed His work in me. If there is one lesson that I am learning day by day, it is this: that it is God who worketh all in all. Oh, that I could help any brother or sister to realize this!

Andrew Murray

Preface

There are three great motives that urge us to humility. It becomes me as a creature, as a sinner, as a saint. The first we see in the heavenly hosts, in unfallen man, in Jesus as Son of Man. The second appeals to us in our fallen states, and points out the only way through which we can return to our right places as creatures. In the third, we have the mystery of grace, which teaches us that as we lose ourselves in the overwhelming greatness of redeeming love, humility becomes to us the consummation of everlasting blessedness and adoration.

In our ordinary religious teaching, the second aspect has been too exclusively put in the foreground, so that some have even gone to the extreme of saying that we must keep sinning if we are indeed to keep humble. Others again have thought that the strength of self-condemnation is the secret of humility. And the Christian life has suffered loss where believers have not been distinctly guided to see that, even in our relations as creatures, nothing is more natural and beautiful and blessed than to be nothing. God may be all. It has not been made clear that it is not sin that humbles most, but grace. It is the soul, led through its sinfulness to be occupied with God in His wonderful glory as God, as Creator and Redeemer, that will truly take the lowest place before Him.

In these meditations I have, for more than one reason, almost exclusively directed attention to the humility that becomes us as creatures. It is not only that the connection between humility and sin is so abundantly set forth in all our religious teaching, but because I believe that for the fullness of the Christian life, it is indispensable that prominence be given to the other aspect.

If Jesus is indeed to be our example in His lowliness, we need to understand the principles in which it was rooted, and in which we find the common ground on which we stand with Him, and in which our likeness to Him is to be attained. If we are indeed to be humble, not only before God but towards men, and if humility is to be our joy, we must see that it is not only the mark of shame, because of sin, but, apart from all sin, a being clothed upon with the very beauty and blessedness of heaven and of Jesus. We shall see that just as Jesus found His glory in taking the form of a servant, so when He said to us, "Whosoever would be first among you, shall be your servant," He simply taught us the blessed truth, that there is nothing so divine and heavenly as being the servant and helper of all.

The faithful servant, who recognizes his position, finds a real pleasure in supplying the wants of the master or his guests. When we see that humility is something infinitely deeper than contrition, and accept it as our participation in the life of Jesus, we shall begin to learn that it is our true nobility, and that to prove it in being servants of all is the highest fulfillment of our destiny, as men created in the image of God.

When I look back upon my own religious experience, or round upon the Church of Christ in the world, I stand amazed at the thought of how little humility is sought as the distinguishing feature of the discipleship of Jesus. In preaching and living, in the daily intercourse of the home and social life, in the more special fellowship with Christians, in the direction and performance of work for Christ. Alas! how much proof there is that humility is not esteemed the cardinal virtue, the only root from which the graces can grow, the one indispensable condition of true fellowship with Jesus. That it should have been possible for men to say of those who claim to be seeking the higher holiness, that the profession has not been accompanied with increasing humility, is a loud call to all earnest Christians, however much or little truth there be in the charge, to prove that meekness and lowliness of heart are the chief marks by which those who follow the meek and lowly Lamb of God are to be known.

"Abide in Jesus. Your life in Him will lead you to that fellowship with God in which the only true knowledge of God is to be had. His love, His power, His infinite glory will, as you abide in Jesus, be so revealed as it hath not entered into the heart of man to conceive."

Andrew Murray
Wellington, South Africa

Biography of Andrew Murray

During the nineteenth century, a number of church revivals swept the world and brought many to Christ who would otherwise never have found Him. In the Dutch Reform Church of South Africa such a revival occurred in the last half of the 1800s. One man stands out as a principle force behind that movement. His name was Andrew Murray. And fortunately for us, not only was he a great preacher and evangelist, he was also a great writer.

Andrew was born in South Africa in 1828. His father and mother were missionaries with the Dutch Reformed Church, having originally emigrated from Scotland. Eventually his father became pastor of a South African church, raising his children in godly fashion, with regular family prayer and hymn singing in the home.

At that time, the first great Christian revival was beginning to move. Andrew's father prayed often for revival to come to his church. Every Friday evening he read to his family accounts of great movements of the Holy Spirit throughout the history of the church. Then he retired to his study to pray, pouring his heart out in tears, pleading with God for a similar outpouring of the Holy Spirit in South Africa.

When Andrew was ten, he and his older brother John were sent to school in Aberdeen, Scotland. There they stayed with their paternal uncle, a well-known minister associated with the Free Church. Their uncle, like their father, was highly interested in the growing revival movement. But unlike South Africa, Scotland was experiencing a series of revivals similar to those taking place in America during the Great Awakening (1795-1835) under Charles Grandison Finney.

Andrew and his brother found themselves in the hub of the movement. Because of his association with the Free Church and his interest in revival, Andrew's uncle frequently had as houseguests the great evangelists and preachers of the day. The young Murray brothers were enthralled by lively conversations on the revival movement and its commitment to a deeper spiritual life.

Close association with men and women of strong faith and intimate knowledge of what God was doing throughout Scotland and America led to the brothers' collective decision to enter the ministry, much to the delight of their uncle and their parents back home in South Africa. So in 1845 the Murray brothers left Scotland for Holland to begin theological studies at the University of Utrecht. Andrew was seventeen at the time.

While in school Andrew made a trip to Germany to see Pastor John Blumhart, who conducted a ministry of healing the sick and casting out demons. Blumhart attributed his success to nothing less than the "experience of the real presence of the Lord Jesus." As he witnessed the healings, Andrew realized that greater power was available to the Church than most Christians realized.

Ironically and in sharp contrast, however, church life in Holland varied from lukewarm to cold. One professor at the university even taught that there are no such things as miracles, that everything could be explained by scientific and natural laws. This way of thinking was part of a new rationalism and formalism that was taking over the Dutch church. But Andrew had already witnessed the miraculous power of God in action. He knew that rationalism and formalism were wrong, and began to seriously question the instruction he was getting at the university.

Fortunately for their growing spiritual life, John and Andrew found a fellowship at the university patterned after the discipleship societies of John Wesley. It was called Zechar Debar (Hebrew for "Remember the Word"). The fellowship worked as a system of "checks and balances" for the brothers. No matter what was taught in the classroom, the Murray's association with this group kept them steadfast and committed to the orthodox biblical theology they had received in South Africa and Scotland.

Disagreement with and departure from classroom theology aside, Andrew came to a deeper realization that he truly belonged to the Lord. He later referred to this as his "conversion." He was also ordained by the Dutch Reform Church after he completed his studies at the age of twenty, the youngest ever to do so.

Following his ordination, he returned to South Africa and was assigned to a small church in the frontier town of Bloemfontein. Covering about 50,000 square miles, his parish had a sparsely scattered population of only 20,000, most of whom were farmers. These Dutch colonists (Boers) had a reputation for fierce independence, and were not easily impressed by outsiders. But even at the age of twenty-one, Andrew so impressed his congregation with his concern and earnest desire to help their families both spiritually and educationally that he was an almost immediate success.

In 1854 he traveled to England on church business. He had been reluctant to leave his parish, but because he had developed a worsening problem with pain in his arms and hands, he decided to leave for a while in order to regain his health. Unfortunately, the rest did not cure his problem, and he had recurrent symptoms throughout the rest of his life.

But the trip was not a complete failure. On his way home he stopped at Cape Town to visit some friends. Originally planning to stay only a few days with them, he changed his mind when he met their daughter Emma. After extending his stay two more weeks, he proposed to her. She turned him down. But Andrew was in love and persistent. He wooed her through letters and several return trips to win her heart. Eventually, she accepted his proposal. They were married in Cape Town on July 2, 1856. Andrew was twenty-eight and Emma, twenty-one.

Emma was a perfect complement to Andrew. She was schooled in music, art, and languages, was widely read, spiritual, pious and social. She would become adept at managing their soon-to-be large and bustling household. The Murrays reared eight children: four sons and four daughters. Not the least of Emma's talents was serving as a buffer between Andrew and all those who would monopolize his time, taking him away from his family and necessary time with God.

Emma also helped Andrew in his work. When he could not write because of the chronic pain in his hands and arms, she took dictation. She also developed many ministries of her own—helping women and their families in need, starting prayer groups, and creating activities for the children of the congregation in support of missionary work. Supporting Andrew, she enjoined his battles against church leaders in Cape Town over the creeping liberalism that was working its way into the Reformed Church.

Interestingly, when revival finally came to his church, Murray resisted it. At first glance, this is difficult to understand. After all, he had grown up in the house of a father who prayed passionately for revival and the house of an uncle who facilitated it and exposed young Andrew to the finest minds of the movement. Murray, himself, had prayed for revival. But when the time came for him to participate, he was held back by his belief that the Holy Spirit only moved through the preaching of the Word, and therefore only through the pastor. He felt unworthy.

He expressed his personal concern in a letter to one of his friends:

> *When I look at my people, my peace forsakes me. I am forced to flee to the Master to seek a new and more entire surrender to His work. My prayer is for revival, but I am held back by the increasing sense of my own unfitness for the work. I lament the awful pride and self-complacency that have now ruled my heart. Oh, that I may be more and more a minister of the Spirit.*

In spite of Murray's personal misgivings, he would not avoid revival for long. Shortly after moving to the geographically smaller and more urban parish of Worchester in 1860, he was introduced to the revival movement in a highly dramatic fashion.

In recounting the event, an associate reported that Murray was finishing a sermon when one of the church elders came running into the sanctuary to tell him that there was a great commotion in the nearby youth meeting hall. Apparently, he reported, a young native girl, standing in the back of the hall during prayer time, had asked if she could share a hymn and pray. Within a short time she was on her knees praying loudly, and soon others in the room joined her in spontaneous song and prayer.

Murray followed his friend to investigate. As they neared the room, the sound grew louder and louder. Murray, confused by thunderous the noise he couldn't identify, opened the door and discovered that all sixty young people were on their knees loudly praying and praising God. They didn't notice their pastor when he entered the room. Deciding that this behavior was inappropriate, he tried to silence them, but they didn't hear him. They continued praying and singing late into the night, finally leaving the church to go out into the streets where others joined them.

At the next church meeting, Murray finished his sermon. As he led everyone in prayer, the members of the congregation—young and old—spontaneously and simultaneously knelt and loudly prayed their own prayers. Again he tried to quiet them, walking up and down the aisle, begging his flock to calm down. But this time a stranger in the back of the church interrupted him, telling the preacher that he had just come from America where he had witnessed the very same thing happening. He told Andrew that he needed to realize that the Spirit of God was at work in his church and that he should do nothing to stop it.

At that moment, the pastor underwent a transformation. He realized that in spite of him, the revival he had been praying for had finally arrived and that he was to be its champion instead of its opponent. To help the movement gain a foothold, Murray traveled around the country preaching about this new thing that was happening. Everywhere he went, revival broke out.

As with any true revival of the Holy Spirit, this was a revival of prayer. People who had seldom been to church in their lives would come to prayer meetings daily and sometimes even more than once a day. And where it had been difficult to find people to join the ministry prior to this time, as the revival spread, young men began stepping forward to offer themselves for the preaching of the Word.

Looking back on these exciting times as well as the lessons of humility that God had taught him, Murray later wrote, "If only we did not so often hinder Him with our much trying to serve. How surely and mightily He would accomplish His own work of renewing souls into the likeness of Jesus Christ."

In 1864, Andrew was made pastor of a large church in Cape Town, where he stayed until 1871. In 1871, probably because of failing health, he transferred to a smaller church in Wellington, forty-five miles away. In many ways this turned out to be very fortunate for both his contemporaries and the generations that have followed; for during his time in Wellington, he began to write down his thoughts about his spiritual experiences and to share his accumulated knowledge on the Holy Spirit working in people's lives.

His books about Church renewal, revival, and the deeper spiritual life flowed from his pen like a river—eventually including over 250 titles, some of which were translated into multiple languages. Many of these reflect his continued theme of the quest for a deeper life in Christ: *The True Vine, Abide in Christ, Absolute Surrender, The Prayer Life, The Lord's Table, How to Raise Your Children for Christ, With Christ in the School of Prayer, Be Perfect.*

In 1879 Murray lost his voice and had to give up preaching. He tried everything he could think of to regain it, but nothing worked. He and Emma moved back to London in 1882, hoping that rest and a change of climate would cure him. His plan was to consult the best physicians in England. But when he returned, he met a minister named Stockmaier who had written several books on healing through prayer. Over the next few weeks, they had several meetings that resulted in Murray checking into a residential healing center in London, and making arrangements to spend time in Bible study and prayer during his stay. Not long after taking up residence there, he attended a healing service during which he was anointed with oil while people prayed over him. His throat was instantly and permanently healed. He and Emma returned to Africa shortly thereafter.

In 1884 he wrote a book called *Divine Healing*, which recounted his experiences and promoted spiritual healing.

It was an instant success. Unfortunately, it turned out to be too much of a good thing for the Dutch Reformed Church. All over South Africa people who had read the book went to their pastors to be healed, only to find that most of the clergy did not believe in healing prayer or have faith strong enough to accomplish it. This problem became so pervasive that the church forced Murray to withdraw the book from publication. It has rarely been published since.

Toward the end of his career, Murray traveled around the world proclaiming the Gospel of Christ and promoting the deeper spiritual life. For a while he joined Moody and Sankey during their evangelistic tour in England. Then afterward he returned with them to the United States where he preached and taught at Moody's school in Northfield, Massachusetts.

After suffering a stroke, Emma died in January of 1905. A year later Andrew retired from the pastorate, but continued on for several more years with his writing, traveling, and preaching. In his later years, however, he rarely ventured from Wellington, where he passed away on January 18, 1917 at the age of 88.

Although his voice was stilled, his ministry lives on in books and treatises that were designed to feed the spiritual hunger of all those who seek a relationship with Jesus Christ. In Murray's work, Christ stands and beckons to us, inviting us to a deeper life with our Maker. You are about to read one of his best and most famous works. There is so much wisdom and richness of thought in *Humility* that it bears reading multiple times; and it is almost a certainty that your understanding of your spiritual journey will be enhanced.

Andrew Murray

1828 - 1917

The house in which Andrew Murray was born,
known as "the old Parsonage," which later became
the home of his son Charles

Andrew Murray's father and mother

Andrew Murray as a young student

Marischal College, Aberdeen

Andrew Murray as
a young minister

John Murray,
Andrew's brother,
as a young minister

The Murray family in 1873.
Andrew is in the back row with his arm
affectionately around his wife Emma

1866 painting of Adderly Street, Cape Town, with the
Dutch Reformed Church in the background

Worcester, South Africa, about 1877.
The town of Andrew Murray's pastorate where great
revival broke out (1860–1864).

Andrew Murray, 43 years old, accepts the call
to the parsonage in the small South African
town of Wellington

Andrew Murray (center) and his family about 1880

Andrew Murray's dwelling, "Clairvaux" (on right)
with the Training Institute for Missionaries (to the left)

Professor Murray age 70

The beach house at Kalk Bay, which Mr. Murray
affectionately called "Patmos"

On the rocks at "Patmos,"
Mr. Murray's favorite place of retreat

Andrew and Emma Murray

Andrew Murray unveiling the monument to his two
colleagues, Professors J. Murray and N. Hofmeyr, 1915

Andrew Murray shortly before his death
on January 18, 1917

CHAPTER 1

Humility: The Glory of the Creature

*Thou art worthy, O Lord, to receive glory and
honour and power: for thou hast created all things,
and for thy pleasure they are and were created
(Revelation 4:11).*

When God created the universe, it was with the one object of making the creature partaker of His perfection and blessedness, and so showing forth in it the glory of His love and wisdom and power. God wished to reveal Himself in and through created beings by communicating to them as much of His own goodness and glory as they were capable of receiving. But this communication was not giving to the creature something which it could possess in itself, a certain life or goodness of which it had the charge and disposal. By no means. But as God is the ever-living, ever-present, ever-acting One, who upholdeth all things by the Word of His power, and in whom all things exist, the relation of the creature to God could only be one of unceasing, absolute, universal dependence.

As truly as God by His power once created, so truly by that same power must God every moment maintain. The creature has only to look back to the origin and first beginning of existence and acknowledge that it there owes everything to God. Its chief care, its highest virtue, and its only happiness, now and through all eternity, are to present itself an empty vessel in which God can dwell and manifest His power and goodness.

The life God bestows is imparted not once for all, but each moment continuously by the unceasing operation of His mighty power. Humility, the place of entire dependence on God, is, from the very nature of things, the first duty and the highest virtue of the creature, and the root of every virtue.

And so pride, or the loss of this humility, is the root of every sin and evil. It was when the now fallen angels began to look upon themselves with self-complacency that they were led to disobedience and were cast down from the light of heaven into outer darkness. Even so, it was when the serpent breathed the poison of his pride, the desire to be as God, into the hearts of our first parents, that they too fell from their high estate into all the wretchedness in which man is now sunk. In heaven and earth, pride and self-exaltation are the gate and the birth and the curse of hell. (See Note at end of chapter.)

Hence it follows that nothing can be our redemption but the restoration of the lost humility, the original and only true relation of the creature to its God. And so Jesus came to bring humility back to earth, to make us partakers of it, and by it to save us. In heaven He humbled Himself to become man. The humility we see in Him possessed

2

Him in heaven; it brought Him, He brought it, from there. Here on earth "He humbled Himself, and became obedient unto death;" His humility gave His death its value, and so became our redemption. And now the salvation He imparts is nothing less and nothing else than a communication of His own life and death, His own disposition and spirit, and His own humility as the ground and root of His relation to God and His redeeming work. Jesus Christ took the place and fulfilled the destiny of man as a creature by His life of perfect humility. His humility is our salvation. His salvation is our humility.

And so the life of the saved ones, of the saints, must bear this stamp of deliverance from sin and full restoration to their original state, their whole relation to God and man marked by an all-pervading humility. Without this there can be no true abiding in God's presence or experience of His favor and the power of His Spirit; without this no abiding faith or love or joy or strength. Humility is the only soil in which the graces root; the lack of humility is the sufficient explanation of every defect and failure. Humility is not so much a grace or virtue along with others; it is the root of all, because it alone takes the right attitude before God, and allows Him as God to do all.

God has so constituted us as reasonable beings, that the truer the insight into the real nature or the absolute need of a command, the readier and fuller will be our obedience to it. The call to humility has been too little regarded in the Church because its true nature and importance have been too little apprehended. It is not a something which we bring to God, or He bestows; it is simply the sense of entire nothingness, which comes when we see how truly God is all, and in which we make way for God to be all. When the creature realizes that this is the true nobility, and consents to be with his will, his mind, and his affections, the form, the vessel in which the life and glory of God are to work and manifest themselves, he sees that humility is simply acknowledging the truth of his position as creature, and yielding to God His place.

In the life of earnest Christians, of those who pursue and profess holiness, humility ought to be the chief mark of their uprightness. It is often said that it is not so. May not one reason be that in the teaching and example of the Church, it has never had that place of supreme importance that belongs to it? And that this, again, is owing to the neglect of this truth, that as strongly as sin is a motive to humility, there is one of still wider and mightier influence: that which makes the angels, that which made Jesus, that which makes the holiest of saints in heaven, so humble; that the first and chief mark of the relation of the creature, the secret of his blessedness, is the humility and nothingness which leave God free to be all?

I am sure there are many Christians who will confess that their experience has been very much like my own in this, that we had long known the Lord without realizing that meekness and lowliness of heart are to be the distinguishing features of the disciple as they were of the Master. And further, that this humility is not a thing that will come of itself, but that it must be made the object of special desire and prayer and faith and practice. As we study the Word, we shall see what very distinct and oft-repeated instructions Jesus gave His disciples on this point, and how slow they were in understanding Him. Let us, at the very commencement of our meditations, admit that there is nothing so natural to man, nothing so insidious and hidden from our sight, nothing so difficult and dangerous as pride. Let us feel that nothing but a very determined and persevering waiting on God and Christ will discover how lacking we are in the grace of humility, and how impotent to obtain what we seek. Let us study the character of Christ until our souls are filled with the love and admiration of His lowliness. And let us believe that when we are broken down under a sense of our pride and our impotence to cast it out, Jesus Christ Himself will come in to impart this grace, too, as a part of His wondrous life within us.

Chapter Endnote

All this is to make it known in the region of eternity that pride can degrade the highest angels into devils, and humility can raise fallen flesh and blood to the thrones of angels. Thus, this is the great end of God raising a new creation out of a fallen kingdom of angels; for this end, it stands in its state of war betwixt the fire and pride of fallen angels, and the humility of the Lamb of God, that the last trumpet may sound the great truth through the depths of eternity, that evil can have no beginning but from pride, and no end but from humility.

The truth is this: Unless pride dies in you, nothing of heaven can live in you. Under the banner of the truth, give yourself up to the meek and humble spirit of the holy Jesus. Humility must sow seed, or there can be no reaping in Heaven. Look not at pride only as an unbecoming temper, nor at humility only as a decent virtue: for the one is death and the other is life; the one is all hell and the other is all heaven. So much as you have of pride within you, you have of the fallen angels alive in you; so much as you have of true humility, so much you have of the Lamb of God within you. Could you see what every stirring of pride does to your soul, you would beg of everything you meet to tear the viper from you, though with the loss of a hand or an eye. Could you see what a sweet, divine, transforming power there is in humility, how it expels the poison of your nature, and makes room for the Spirit of God to live in you, you would rather wish to be the footstool of all the world than want the smallest degree of it.

– *Spirit of Prayer*, Pt.II, p.73, Edition of Moreton, Canterbury, 1893.

CHAPTER 2

Humility: The Secret of Redemption

Have this mind be in you, which was also in Christ Jesus, being in the form of God, thought it not robbery to be equal with God: But made himself of no reputation, and took upon him the form of a servant, and was made in the likeness of men: And being found in fashion as a man, he humbled himself, and became obedient unto death, even the death of the cross. Wherefore God also hath highly exalted him, and given him a name which is above every name (Philippians 2:5-9).

No tree can grow except on the root from which it sprang. Through all its existence it can only live with the life that was in the seed that gave it being. The full apprehension of this truth in its application to the first and the Second Adam cannot but help us greatly to understand the need and the nature of the redemption there is in Jesus.

When the Old Serpent, he who had been cast out from heaven for his pride, whose whole nature as devil was pride, spoke his words of temptation into the ear of Eve, these words carried with them the very poison of hell. And when she listened and yielded her desire and her will to the prospect of being as God, knowing good and evil, the poison entered into her soul and blood and life, destroying forever that blessed humility and dependence upon God, which would have been our everlasting happiness. Her life and the life of the race that sprang from her became corrupted to its very root with that most terrible of all sins and all curses, the poison of Satan's own pride. All the wretchedness of which this world has been the scene, all its wars and bloodshed among the nations, all its selfishness and suffering, all its ambitions and jealousies, all its broken hearts and embittered lives, and all its daily unhappiness have their origin in what this cursed, hellish pride, either our own or that of others, has brought us. It is pride that made redemption needful. It is from our pride we need above everything to be redeemed. And our insight into the need of redemption will largely depend upon our knowledge of the terrible nature of the power that has entered our being.

No tree can grow except on the root from which it sprang. The power that Satan brought from hell and cast into man's life is working daily, hourly with mighty power throughout the world. Men suffer from it; they fear and fight and flee it; and yet they know not whence it comes, whence it has its terrible supremacy. No wonder they do not know where or how it is to be overcome. Pride has its root and strength in a terrible spiritual power, outside of us as well as within us; as needful as it is that we confess and deplore it as our very own, is to know it in its Satanic origin. If this leads us to utter despair of ever conquering or casting it out, it will lead us all the sooner to that supernatural power in which alone our deliverance is to be found—the redemption of the Lamb of God. The hopeless struggle against the workings of self and pride within us may indeed become still more hopeless as we think of the power of darkness behind it all. The utter despair will fit us the better for realizing and accepting a power and a life outside of ourselves, too, even the humility of heaven as brought down and brought nigh by the Lamb of God to cast out Satan and his pride.

No tree can grow except on the root from which it sprang. Even as we need to look to the first Adam and his fall to know the power of the sin within us, we need to know well the Second Adam and His power to give within us a life of humility as real and abiding and overmastering as has been that of pride. We have our life from and in Christ, as truly, yea more truly, than from and in Adam. We are to walk "rooted in Him," "holding fast the Head from whom the whole body increaseth with the increase of God." The life of God, which in the incarnation entered human nature, is the root in which we are to stand and grow. It is the same almighty power that worked there and thence onward to the resurrection, which works daily in us. Our one need is to study and know and trust the life that has been revealed in Christ as the life that is now ours, and waits for our consent to gain possession and mastery of our whole being.

In this view, it is inconceivably important that we should have right thoughts of what Christ is, of what really constitutes Him the Christ, and especially of what may be counted His chief characteristic, the root and essence of all His character as our Redeemer. There can be but one answer. It is His humility. What is the incarnation but His heavenly humility, His emptying Himself and becoming man? What is His life on earth but humility, His taking the form of a servant? And what is His atonement but humility? "He humbled Himself and became obedient unto death." And what are His ascension and His glory but humility exalted to the throne and crowned with glory? "He humbled Himself, therefore God highly exalted Him." In heaven, where He was with the Father, in His birth, in His life, in His death, in His sitting on the throne, it is all; it is nothing but humility.

Christ is the humility of God embodied in human nature: the Eternal Love humbling itself, clothing itself in the garb of meekness and gentleness, to win and serve and save us. As the love and condescension of God makes Him the benefactor and helper and servant of all, so Jesus of necessity was the Incarnate Humility. And so He is still in the midst of the throne, the meek and lowly Lamb of God.

If this were the root of the tree, its nature must be seen in every branch and leaf and fruit. If humility is the first, all-including grace of the life of Jesus, if humility is the secret of His atonement, then the health and strength of our spiritual life will entirely depend upon our putting this grace first, too, and making humility the chief thing we admire in Him, the chief thing we ask of Him, the one thing for which we sacrifice all else. (See Note at end of this chapter.)

Is it any wonder that the Christian life is so often feeble and fruitless, when the very root of the Christ life is neglected or unknown? Is it any wonder that the joy of salvation is so little felt, when that in which Christ found it and brings it, is so little sought? Until a humility which will rest in nothing less than the end and death of self; which gives up all the honor of men as Jesus did, to seek the honor that comes from God alone; which absolutely makes and counts itself nothing, that God may be all, that the Lord alone may be exalted, until such a humility be what we seek in Christ above our chief joy, and welcome at any price, there is very little hope of a religion that will conquer the world.

I cannot too earnestly plead with my reader, if possibly his attention has never yet been specially directed to the lack of humility within him or around him, to pause and ask whether he sees much of the spirit of the meek and lowly Lamb of God in those who are called by His name. Let him consider how all want of love; all indifference to the needs, the feelings, the weakness of others; all sharp and hasty judgments and utterances, so often excused under the plea of being outright and honest; all manifestations of temper and touchiness and irritation; and all feelings of bitterness and estrangement have their roots in nothing but pride, that ever seeks itself. And his eyes will be opened to see how a dark, shall I not say a devilish, pride creeps in almost everywhere, the assemblies of the saints not excepted. Let him begin to ask what would be the effect if in himself and around him, if towards fellow saints and the world, believers were really permanently guided by the humility of Jesus; and let him say if the cry of our whole heart, night and day, ought not to be, Oh for the humility of Jesus in myself and all around me! Let him honestly fix his heart on his own lack of the humility, which has been revealed in the likeness of Christ's life, and in the whole character of His redemption, and he will begin to

11

feel as if he had never yet really known what Christ and His salvation are.

Believer, study the humility of Jesus! This is the secret, the hidden root of thy redemption. Sink down into it deeper day by day. Believe with thy whole heart that this Christ, whom God has given thee, even as His divine humility wrought the work for thee, will enter in to dwell and work within thee, too, and make thee what the Father would have thee be.

Chapter Endnote

We need to know two things:

1. That our salvation consists wholly in being saved from ourselves, or that which we are by nature;

2. That in the whole nature of things, nothing could be this salvation or savior to us but such a humility of God as is beyond all expression.

Hence the first unalterable term of the Savior to fallen man: Except a man denies himself, he cannot be My disciple. Self is the whole evil of fallen nature; self-denial is our capacity of being saved; humility is our savior ... Self is the root, the branches, the tree, of all the evil of our fallen state. All the evils of fallen angels and men have their birth in the pride of self. On the other hand, all the virtues of the heavenly life are the virtues of humility. It is humility alone that makes the unpassable gulf between heaven and hell.

What is then, or in what lies the great struggle for eternal life? It all lies in the strife between pride and humility: pride and humility are the two master powers, the two kingdoms in strife for the eternal possession of man. There never was, nor ever will be, but one humility, and that is the one humility of Christ. Pride and self have the all of man, till man has his all from Christ. He therefore only fights the good fight whose strife is that the self-idolatrous nature which he hath from Adam may be brought to death by the supernatural humility of Christ brought to life in him.

–W. Law, *Address to the Clergy*, p. 52.

CHAPTER 3

Humility in the Life of Jesus

... I am among you as he that serveth (Luke 22:27).

In the Gospel of John we have the inner life of our Lord laid open to us. Jesus speaks frequently of His relation to the Father, of the motives by which He is guided, of His consciousness of the power and spirit in which He acts. Though the word "humble" does not occur, we shall nowhere in Scripture see more clearly wherein His humility consisted.

We have already said that this grace is in truth nothing but that simple consent of the creature to let God be all, in virtue of which it surrenders itself to His working alone. In Jesus we shall see how both as the Son of God in heaven, and as man upon earth, He took the place of entire subordination, and gave God the honor and the glory, which is due to Him. And what He taught so often was made true to Himself: "He that humbleth him shall be exalted." As it is written, "He humbled Himself, therefore God highly exalted Him."

Listen to the words in which our Lord speaks of His relation to the Father, and how unceasingly He uses the words *not* and *nothing* in reference to Himself. The "not I" in which Paul expresses his relation to Christ is the very spirit of what Christ says of His relation to the Father.

"... *The Son can do nothing of himself* ..." *(John 5:19).*

"*I can of mine own self do nothing: as I hear, I judge: and my judgment is just; because I seek not mine own will, but the will of the Father which hath sent me*" *(John 5:30).*

"*I receive not honour from men*" *(John 5:41).*

"*For I came down from heaven, not to do mine own will, but the will of him that sent me*" *(John 6:38).*

"*Jesus answered them, and said, My doctrine is not mine, but his that sent me*" *(John 7:16).*

"... *I am not come of myself* ..." *(John 7:28).*

"... *I do nothing of myself; but as my Father hath taught me, I speak these things*" *(John 8:28).*

"... *neither came I of myself, but he sent me*" *(John 8:42).*

"*And I seek not mine own glory: there is one that seeketh and judgeth*" *(John 8:50).*

"... *the words that I speak unto you I speak not of myself: but the Father that dwelleth in me, he doeth the works*" *(John 14:10).*

16

"… the word which ye hear is not mine, but the Father's which sent me" (John 14:24).

These words open to us the deepest roots of Christ's life and work. They tell us how it was that the Almighty God was able to work His mighty redemptive work through Him. They show what Christ counted the state of heart, which became Him as the Son of the Father. They teach us what the essential nature and life is of that redemption, which Christ accomplished and now communicates. It is this: He was nothing, that God might be all. He resigned Himself with His will and His powers entirely for the Father to work in Him. Of His own power, His own will, and His own glory, of His whole mission with all His works and His teaching, of all this He said, *It is not I. I am nothing; I have given Myself to the Father to work. I am nothing; the Father is all.*

This life of entire self-abnegation, of absolute submission and dependence upon the Father's will, Christ found to be one of perfect peace and joy. He lost nothing by giving all to God. God honored His trust, and did all for Him, and then exalted Him to His own right hand in glory. And because Christ had thus humbled Himself before God, and God was ever before Him, He found it possible to humble Himself before men, too, and to be the Servant of all. His humility was simply the surrender of Himself to God, to allow Him to do in Him what He pleased, whatever men around might say of Him or do to Him.

It is in this state of mind, in this spirit and disposition, that the redemption of Christ has its virtue and efficacy. It is to bring us to this disposition that we are made partakers of Christ. This is the true self-denial to which our Saviour calls us: the acknowledgment that self has nothing good in it, except as an empty vessel which God must fill, and that its claim to be or do anything may not for a moment be allowed. It is in this, above and before everything, in which the conformity to Jesus consists, the being and doing nothing of ourselves, that God may be all.

Here we have the root and nature of true humility. It is because this is not understood or sought that our humility is so superficial and so feeble. We must learn of Jesus, how He is meek and lowly of heart. He teaches us where true humility takes its rise and finds its strength—in the knowledge that it is God who worketh all in all, that our place is to yield to Him in perfect resignation and dependence, in full consent to be and to do nothing of ourselves. This is the life Christ came to reveal and to impart—a life to God that came through death to sin and self.

If we feel that this life is too high for us and beyond our reach, it must but the more urge us to seek it in Him. It is the indwelling Christ who will live in us this life, meek and lowly. If we long for this, let us, meantime and above everything, seek the holy secret of the knowledge of the nature of God, as He every moment works all in all; the secret, of which all nature and every creature, and above all, every child of God, is to be the witness: that it is nothing but a vessel, a channel through which the living God can manifest the riches of His wisdom, power, and goodness. The root of all virtue and grace, of all faith and acceptable worship, is that we know that we have nothing except that which we receive, and bow in deepest humility to wait upon God for it.

It was because this humility was not only a temporary sentiment, awakened and brought into exercise when He thought of God, but the very spirit of His whole life, that Jesus was just as humble in His intercourse with men as with God. He felt Himself the Servant of God for the men whom God made and loved. As a natural consequence, He counted Himself the Servant of men, that through Him God might do His work of love.

He never for a moment thought of seeking His honor or asserting His power to vindicate Himself. His whole spirit was that of a life yielded to God to work in. It is not until Christians study the humility of Jesus as the very essence of His redemption, as the very blessedness of the life of the Son of God, as the only true relation to the Father, and therefore as that which Jesus must give us if we are to have any part with Him, that the terrible lack of actual, heavenly, manifest humility will become a burden and a sorrow, and our ordinary religion be set aside to secure this, the first and the chief of the marks of the Christ within us.

Brother, are you clothed with humility? Ask your daily life. Ask Jesus. Ask your friends. Ask the world. And begin to praise God that there is opened up to you in Jesus a heavenly humility of which you have hardly known, and through which a heavenly blessedness you possibly have never yet tasted can come in to you.

CHAPTER 4

Humility in the Teaching of Jesus

*Take my yoke upon you, and learn of me; for I am
meek and lowly in heart: and ye shall find rest unto
your souls (Matthew 11:29).*

We have seen humility in the life of Christ, as He
lay open His heart to us. Let us listen to His
teaching. There we shall hear how He speaks
of it, and how far He expects men, and specially His
disciples, to be humble as He was. Let us carefully study
the passages, which I can scarce do more than quote, to
receive the full impression of how often and how earnestly
He taught it. It may help us to realize what He asks of us.

1. Look at the commencement of His ministry. In the
Beatitudes with which the Sermon on the Mount opens,
He speaks: "Blessed are the poor in spirit; for theirs is the
kingdom of heaven. Blessed are the meek; for they shall
inherit the earth." The very first words of His proclamation
of the kingdom of heaven reveal the open gate through

which alone we enter. The poor, who have nothing in themselves, to them the kingdom comes. The meek, who seek nothing in themselves, theirs the earth shall be. The blessings of heaven and earth are for the lowly. For the heavenly and the earthly life, humility is the secret of blessing.

2. *"Take my yoke upon you, and learn of me; for I am meek and lowly in heart: and ye shall find rest unto your souls" (Matthew 11:29).* Jesus offers Himself as Teacher. He tells what the spirit both is, which we shall find Him as Teacher, and which we can learn and receive from Him. We shall find perfect rest in the one thing He offers us: meekness and lowliness. Humility is to be a salvation.

3. The disciples had been disputing who would be the greatest in the kingdom, and had agreed to ask the Master (Luke 9:46, Matthew 18:3). He set a child in their midst and said, *"Whosoever therefore shall humble himself as this little child, the same is greatest in the kingdom of heaven" (Matthew 18:4).* **Who would be the greatest in the kingdom of heaven?** The question is indeed a far-reaching one. **What will be the chief distinction in the heavenly kingdom?** The answer, none but Jesus would have given. The chief glory of heaven, the true heavenly-mindedness, the chief of the graces is humility. *"For he who is least among you all—he is the greatest" (Luke 9:48).*

4. The sons of Zebedee had asked Jesus if they could sit on His right and left, the highest place in the kingdom. Jesus said it was not His to give, but the Father's, who would give it to those for whom it was prepared. They must not look or ask for it. Their thought must be of the cup and the baptism of humiliation. And then He added,

"And whosoever will be chief among you, let him be your servant: Even as the Son of man came not to be ministered unto, but to minister, and to give his life a ransom for many" (Matthew 20:27-28). Humility, as it is the mark of Christ the heavenly, will be the one standard of glory in heaven: the lowliest is the nearest to God. The primacy in the Church is promised to the most humble.

5. Speaking to the multitude and the disciples, of the Pharisees and their love of the chief seats, Christ said once again (Matthew 23:11), *"He that is greatest among you shall be your servant."* Humiliation is the only ladder to honor in God's kingdom.

6. On another occasion, in the house of a Pharisee, He spoke the parable of the guest who would be invited to come up higher (Luke 14:1-11), and added, *"For whosoever exalteth himself shall be abased; and he that humbleth himself shall be exalted."* The demand is inexorable; there is no other way. Self-abasement alone will be exalted.

7. After the parable of the Pharisee and the Publican, Christ spake again (Luke 18:14), *"Everyone that exalteth himself shall be abased; and he that humbleth himself shall be exalted."* In the temple and presence and worship of God, everything is worthless that is not pervaded by deep, true humility towards God and men.

8. After washing the disciples' feet, Jesus said (John 13:14), *"If I then, the Lord and Master, have washed your feet, ye also ought to wash one another's feet."* The authority of command, and example, every thought, either

of obedience or conformity, make humility the first and most essential element of discipleship.

9. At the Holy Supper table, the disciples still disputed who should be greatest (Luke 22:26). Jesus said, *"But ye shall not be so: but he that is greatest among you, let him be as the younger; and he that is chief, as he that doth serve" (Luke 22:26).* The path in which Jesus walked, and which He opened up for us, the power and spirit in which He wrought out salvation, and to which He saves us, is ever the humility that makes me the servant of all.

How little this is preached. How little it is practiced. How little the lack of it is felt or confessed. I do not say, how few attain to it, some recognizable measure of likeness to Jesus in His humility. But how few ever think of making it a distinct object of continual desire or prayer. How little the world has seen it. How little has it been seen even in the inner circle of the Church.

"Whosoever will be chief among you, let him be your servant." Would God that it might be given us to believe that Jesus means this! We all know what the character of a faithful servant or slave implies. Devotion to the master's interests, thoughtful study and care to please him, delight in his prosperity and honor and happiness. There are servants on earth in whom these dispositions have been seen, and to whom the name of servant has never been anything but a glory. To how many of us has it not been a new joy in the Christian life to know that we may yield ourselves as servants, as slaves to God, and to find that His service is our highest liberty, the liberty from sin and self?

We need now to learn another lesson: that Jesus calls us to be servants of one another, and that, as we accept it heartily, this service, too, will be a most blessed one, a new and fuller liberty, too, from sin and self. At first it may appear hard; this is only because of the pride, which still counts itself something. If once we learn that to be nothing before God is the glory of the creature, the spirit of Jesus, the joy of heaven, we shall welcome with our whole hearts the discipline we may have in serving even those who try to vex us.

When our own hearts are set upon this, the true sanctification, we shall study each word of Jesus on self-abasement with new zest, and no place will be too low, no stooping too deep, and no service too mean or too long continued, if we may but share and prove the fellowship with Him who spake, "I am among you as he that serveth."

Brethren, here is the path to the higher life. Down, lower down! This was what Jesus always said to the disciples who were thinking of being great in the kingdom and of sitting on His right hand and His left. Seek not; ask not for exaltation. That is God's work. Look to it that you abase and humble yourselves, and take no place before God or man but that of servant; that is your work; let that be your one purpose and prayer. God is faithful. Just as water ever seeks and fills the lowest place, so the moment God finds the creature abased and empty, His glory and power flow in to exalt and to bless. He that humbleth himself—that must be our one care—shall be exalted; that is God's care. By His mighty power and in His great love He will do it.

Men sometimes speak as if humility and meekness would rob us of that which is noble and bold and manlike. Oh, that all would believe that this is the nobility of the kingdom of heaven, that this is the royal spirit that the King of heaven displayed, that this is Godlike, to humble oneself, to become the servant of all! This is the path to the gladness and the glory of Christ's presence ever in us, His power ever resting on us.

Jesus, the meek and lowly One, calls us to learn of Him the path to God. Let us study the words we have been reading, until our heart is filled with the thought: My one need is humility. And let us believe that what He shows, He gives; what He is, He imparts. As the meek and lowly One, He will come in and dwell in the longing heart.

CHAPTER 5

Humility in the Disciples of Jesus

*But ye shall not be so: but he that is greatest among
you, let him be as the younger; and he that is chief,
as he that doth serve (Luke 22:26).*

We have studied humility in the person and
teaching of Jesus; let us now look for it in the
circle of His chosen companions—the twelve
apostles. If, in the lack of it we find in them, the contrast
between Christ and men is brought out more clearly, it
will help us to appreciate the mighty change which
Pentecost wrought in them, and prove how real our
participation can be in the perfect triumph of Christ's
humility over the pride Satan had breathed into man.

In the texts quoted from the teaching of Jesus, we have
already seen the occasions on which the disciples proved
how entirely wanting they were in the grace of humility.
Once, they had been disputing the way which of them
should be the greatest. Another time, the sons of Zebedee

with their mother had asked for the first places—the seat on the right hand and the left. And, later on, at the Supper table on the last night, there was again a contention over which man should be accounted the greatest. Not that there were not moments when they indeed humbled themselves before their Lord. So it was with Peter when he cried out, *"... Depart from me; for I am a sinful man, O Lord" (Luke 5:8)*. So, too, with the disciples when they fell down and worshipped Him who had stilled the storm. But such occasional expressions of humility only bring out into stronger relief the habitual tone of their mind, as shown in the natural and spontaneous revelation given at other times of the place and the power of self. The study of the meaning of all this will teach us most important lessons.

First. How much there may be of earnest and active religion while humility is still sadly wanting. See it in the disciples. There was in them fervent attachment to Jesus. They had forsaken all for Him. The Father had revealed to them that He was the Christ of God. They believed in Him; they loved Him; they obeyed His commandments. They had forsaken all to follow Him. When others went back, they clave to Him. They were ready to die with Him. But deeper down than all this, there was a dark power, of the existence and the hideousness of which they were hardly conscious, which had to be slain and cast out, ere they could be the witnesses of the power of Jesus to save. It is even so still.

We may find professors and ministers, evangelists and workers, missionaries and teachers in whom the gifts of the Spirit are many and manifest, and who are the channels of blessing to multitudes, but of whom, when the testing time comes, or closer intercourse gives fuller knowledge, it is only too painfully manifest that the grace of humility, as an abiding characteristic, is scarce to be seen. All tends to confirm the lesson that humility is one of the chief and the highest graces, one of the most difficult of attainment, one to which our first and chiefest efforts ought to be directed, one that only comes in power when the fullness of the Spirit makes us partakers of the indwelling Christ, and He lives within us.

Second. How impotent all external teaching and all personal effort are to conquer pride or give the meek and lowly heart. For three years the disciples had been in the training school of Jesus. He had told them what the chief lesson was He wished to teach them: *"Take my yoke upon you, and learn of me; for I am meek and lowly in heart: and ye shall find rest unto your souls"* *(Matthew 11:29).* Time after time He had spoken to them, to the Pharisees, to the multitude of humility as the only path to the glory of God. He had not only lived before them as the Lamb of God in His divine humility, He had more than once unfolded to them the inmost secret of His life: *"For even the Son of Man came not to be ministered to, but to minister ..."* *(Mark 10:45).* *"For whether is greater, he that sitteth at meat, or he that serveth? is not he that sitteth at meat? but I am among you as he that serveth"* *(Luke 22:27).* He had washed their feet and told them they were to follow His example. And yet all had availed but little. At the Holy Supper there was still the contention as to who should be greatest.

They had doubtless often tried to learn His lessons, and firmly resolved not to grieve Him again. But all in vain. To teach them and us the much needed lesson, that no outward instruction, not even of Christ Himself; no argument however convincing; no sense of the beauty of humility, however deep; no personal resolve or effort, however sincere and earnest, can cast out the devil of pride. When Satan casts out Satan, it is only to enter afresh in a mightier, more hidden power. Nothing can avail but this, that the new nature in its divine humility be revealed in power to take the place of the old, to become as truly our very nature as that ever was.

Third. It is only by the indwelling of Christ in His divine humility that we become truly humble. We have our pride from another, from Adam. We must have our humility from Another, too. Pride is ours, and rules in us with such terrible power, because it is ourselves, our very nature. Humility must be ours in the same way; it must be our very self, our very nature. As natural and easy as it has been to be proud, it must be, it will be, to be humble. The promise is, "Where," even in the heart, "sin abounded, grace did abound more exceedingly." All Christ's teaching of His disciples and all their vain efforts were the needful preparation for His entering into them in divine power, to give and be in them what He had taught them to desire.

In His death He destroyed the power of the devil, He put away sin, and affected an everlasting redemption. In His resurrection He received from the Father an entirely new life, the life of man in the power of God, capable of being communicated to men, and entering and renewing and filling their lives with His divine power. In His ascension He received the Spirit of the Father, through whom He might do what He could not do while upon earth: make Himself one with those He loved, actually live their life for them, so that they could live before the Father in a humility like His, because it was Himself who lived and breathed in them. And on Pentecost He came and took possession. The work of preparation and conviction, the awakening of desire and hope that His teaching had affected, was perfected by the mighty change that Pentecost wrought. The lives and the epistles of James, Peter, and John bear witness that all was changed, and that the spirit of the meek and suffering Jesus had indeed possession of them.

What shall we say to these things? Among my readers I am sure there is more than one class. There may be some who have never yet thought very specially of the matter, and cannot at once realize its immense importance as a life question for the Church and its every member. There are others who have felt condemned for their shortcomings, and have put forth very earnest efforts, only to fail and be discouraged. Others, again, may be able to give joyful testimony of spiritual blessing and power. Yet there has never been the needed conviction of what those around them still see as wanting. And still others may be able to witness that in regard to this grace, too, the Lord has given deliverance and victory, while He has taught them how much they still need and may expect out of the fullness of Jesus.

To whichever class we belong, may I urge the pressing need there is for our all seeking a still deeper conviction of the unique place that humility holds in the religion of Christ, and the utter impossibility of the Church or the believer being what Christ would have them be, as long as His humility is not recognized as His chief glory, His first command, and our highest blessedness. Let us consider deeply how far the disciples were advanced while this grace was still so terribly lacking, and let us pray to God that

31

other gifts may not so satisfy us, that we never grasp the fact that the absence of this grace is the secret cause why the power of God cannot do its mighty work. It is only where we, like the Son, truly know and show that we can do nothing of ourselves, that God will do all.

It is when the truth of an indwelling Christ takes the place it claims in the experience of believers, that the Church will put on her beautiful garments, and humility will be seen in her teachers and members as the beauty of holiness.

CHAPTER 6

Humility in Daily Life

If a man say, I love God, and hateth his brother,
he is a liar: for he that loveth not his brother whom
he hath seen, how can he love God whom he hath
not seen? (1 John 4:20)

What a solemn thought, that our love to God will be measured by our everyday intercourse with men and the love it displays; and that our love to God will be found to be a delusion, except as its truth is proved in standing the test of daily life with our fellow men. It is even so with our humility. It is easy to think we humble ourselves before God. Humility towards men will be the only sufficient proof that our humility before God is real, that humility has taken up its abode in us and become our very nature, and that we actually, like Christ, have made ourselves of no reputation. When in the presence of God lowliness of heart has become not a posture we pray to Him, but the very spirit of our life, it will manifest itself in all our bearing towards our brethren. The lesson is one of deep import: the only humility that is really ours is not that which we try to show before God in prayer, but that which we carry with us, and carry out in our ordinary conduct—the insignficances of daily life are the importances and the tests of eternity, because they prove what really is the spirit that possesses us. It is in our most unguarded moments that we really show and see what we are. To know the humble man and to know how the humble man behaves, you must follow him in the common course of daily life.

Is not this what Jesus taught? It was when the disciples disputed who should be greatest, when He saw how the Pharisees loved the chief place at feasts and the chief seats in the synagogues and when He had given them the example of washing their feet that He taught His lessons of humility. Humility before God is nothing if not proved in humility before men.

It is even so in the teaching of Paul. To the Romans he writes, *"Be of the same mind one toward another. Mind not high things, but condescend to men of low estate. Be not wise in your own conceits"* (Romans 12:16).

To the Corinthians: *"Charity,"* and there is no love without humility as its root, *"suffereth long, and is kind; charity envieth not; charity vaunteth not itself, is not puffed up ..."* (1 Corinthians 13:4).

To the Galatians: *"Let us not be desirous of vain glory, provoking one another, envying one another"* (Galatians 5:26).

To the Ephesians, immediately after the three wonderful chapters on the heavenly life: "*With all lowliness and meekness, with longsuffering, forbearing one another in love ...*" *(Ephesians 4:2)*. "*Giving thanks always for all things unto God and the Father in the name of our Lord Jesus Christ ...*" *(Ephesians 5:20)*.

To the Philippians: "*Let nothing be done through strife or vainglory; but in lowliness of mind let each esteem other better than themselves. Look not every man on his own things, but every man also on the things of others. Let this mind be in you, which was also in Christ Jesus ...*" *(Philippians 2:3-5)*.

And to the Colossians: "*Forbearing one another, and forgiving one another, if any man have a quarrel against any: even as Christ forgave you, so also do ye*" *(Colossians 3:13)*.

It is in our relation to one another and in our treatment of one another that the true lowliness of mind and the heart of humility are to be seen. Our humility before God has no value except as it prepares us to reveal the humility of Jesus to our fellow men. Let us study humility in daily life in the light of these words.

The humble man seeks at all times to act up to the rule, "In honor preferring one another; Servants one of another; Each counting others better than himself Subjecting yourselves one to another."

The question is often asked, how we can count others better than ourselves, when we see that they are far below us in wisdom and in holiness, in natural gifts, or in grace received. The question proves at once how little we understand what real lowliness of mind is. True humility comes when, in the light of God, we have seen ourselves to be nothing, have consented to part with and cast away self, and to let God be all.

The soul that has done this can say, *So have I lost myself in finding Thee*, and no longer compares itself with others. It has given up forever every thought of self in God's presence; it meets its fellow men as one who is nothing and seeks nothing for itself; it is a servant of God, and for His sake, a servant of all. A faithful servant may be wiser than the master, and yet retain the true spirit and posture of the servant. The humble man looks upon every, the feeblest and unworthiest, child of God, and honors him and prefers him in honor as the son of a King. The spirit of Him, who washed the disciples' feet, makes it a joy for us to be indeed the least, to be servants one of another.

The humble man feels no jealousy or envy. He can praise God when others are preferred and blessed before him. He can bear to hear others praised and himself forgotten, because in God's presence he has learnt to say with Paul, "I am nothing." He has received the spirit of Jesus, who pleased not Himself, and sought not His own honor, as the spirit of his life.

Amid what are considered the temptations to impatience and touchiness, to hard thoughts and sharp words, which come from the failings and sins of fellow-Christians, the humble man carries the oftrepeated injunction in his heart, and shows it in his life: *"Forbearing one another, and forgiving one another, if any man have a quarrel against any: even as Christ forgave you, so also do ye" (Colossians 3:13).* He has learnt that in putting on the

Lord Jesus, he has put on the heart of compassion, kindness, humility, meekness, and long-suffering. Jesus has taken the place of self, and it is not an impossibility to forgive as Jesus forgave. His humility does not consist merely in thoughts or words of self-deprecation, but, as Paul puts it, in "a heart of humility," encompassed by compassion and kindness, meekness and longsuffering, the sweet and lowly gentleness recognized as the mark of the Lamb of God.

In striving after the higher experiences of the Christian life, the believer is often in danger of aiming at and rejoicing in what one might call the more human, the manly virtues, such as boldness, joy, contempt of the world, zeal, and self-sacrifice. Even the old Stoics taught and practiced these, while the deeper and gentler, the more divine and heavenly graces, those which Jesus first taught upon earth, because He brought them from heaven; those which are more distinctly connected with His cross and the death of self, poverty of spirit, meekness, humility, and lowliness are scarcely thought of or valued. Therefore, let us put on a heart of compassion, kindness, humility, meekness, long-suffering. Let us prove our Christlikeness, not only in our zeal for saving the lost, but before all in our intercourse with the brethren, forbearing and forgiving one another, even as the Lord forgave us.

Fellow Christians, do let us study the Bible portrait of the humble man. And let us ask our brethren, and the world whether or not they recognize in us the likeness to the original. Let us be content with nothing less than taking each of these texts as the promise of what God will work in us, as the revelation in words of what the Spirit of Jesus will give as a birth within us. And let each failure and shortcoming simply urge us to turn humbly and meekly to the meek and lowly Lamb of God in the assurance that where He is enthroned in the heart, His humility and gentleness will be one of the streams of living water that flow from within us.

I knew Jesus, and He was very precious to my soul; but I found something in me that would not keep sweet and patient and kind. I did what I could to keep it down, but it was there. I besought Jesus to do something for me, and when I gave Him my will, He came to my heart, and took out all that would not be sweet, all that would not be kind, all that would not be patient, and then He shut the door. – George Foxe

Once again I repeat what I have said before. I feel deeply that we have very little conception of what the Church suffers from the lack of this divine humility, the nothingness that makes room for God to prove His power.

Not long ago, a Christian, a man with a loving and humble spirit and acquainted with not a few mission stations in various societies, expressed deep sorrow that in some cases, the spirits of love and forbearance were sadly lacking. Men and women, who in Europe could each choose their own circle of friends and brought close together with others of uncongenial minds, find it hard to bear and to love and to keep the unity of the Spirit in the bond of peace. And those who should have been fellow-helpers of each other's joy became a hindrance and a weariness. And all for the one reason: the lack of the humility, which counts itself nothing, rejoices in becoming and being counted the least, and only seeks, like Jesus, to be the servant, the helper and comforter of others, even the lowest and unworthiest.

And whence comes it that men, who have joyfully given up themselves for Christ, find it so hard to give up themselves for their brethren? Is not the blame with the Church? It has so little taught its sons that the humility of Christ is the first of the virtues, the best of all the graces and powers of the Spirit. It has so little proved that a Christlike humility is what it, like Christ, places and preaches first, as what is in very deed needed and possible, too. But let us not be discouraged. Let the discovery of the lack of this grace stir us to larger expectation from God. Let us look upon every brother who tries or vexes us as God's means of grace, God's instrument for our purification, and our exercise of the humility Jesus, our Life, breathes within us. And let us have such faith in the All of God and the nothing of self that, as nothing in our own eyes, we may seek only to serve one another in love in God's power.

CHAPTER 7

Humility and Holiness

Which say, Stand by thyself, come not near to me;
for I am holier than thou (Isaiah 65:5).

*W*e speak of the holiness movement in our times,
and praise God for it. We hear a great deal of
seekers after holiness and professors of holiness,
of holiness teaching and holiness meetings. The blessed
truths of holiness in Christ and holiness by faith are being
emphasized as never before. The great test of whether or
not the holiness we profess to seek or to attain, truth and
life, will be manifest in the increasing humility it produces.
In the creature, humility is the one thing needed to allow
God's holiness to dwell in him and shine through him. In
Jesus, the Holy One of God who makes us holy, a divine
humility was the secret of His life and His death and His
exaltation. The one infallible test of our holiness will be
the humility before God and men which marks us. Humility
is the bloom and the beauty of holiness.

The chief mark of counterfeit holiness is its lack of humility. Every seeker after holiness needs to be on his guard, lest unconsciously that which was begun in the spirit is perfected in the flesh, and pride creep in where its presence is least expected.

Two men went up into the temple to pray: the one a Pharisee, the other a publican. There is no place or position so sacred but the Pharisee can enter there. Pride can lift its head in the very temple of God, and make His worship the scene of its self-exaltation. Since the time Christ so exposed his pride, the Pharisee has put on the garb of the publican. So the confessor of deep sinfulness must be as on watch as the professor of the highest holiness. Just when we are most anxious to have our hearts the temple of God, we shall find the two men coming up to pray. And the publican will find that his danger is not from the Pharisee beside him, who despises him, but the Pharisee within who commends and exalts. In God's temple, when we think we are in the holiest of all, in the presence of His holiness, let us beware of pride. "Now there was a day when the sons of God came to present themselves before the Lord, and Satan came also among them."

"God, I thank thee, I am not as the rest of men, or even as this publican." It is in that which is just cause for thanksgiving, it is in the very thanksgiving which we render to God, it may be in the very confession that God has done it all, that self finds its cause of complacency. Yes, even in the temple, when the language of penitence and trust in God's mercy alone is heard, the Pharisee may take up the note of praise, and in thanking God, be congratulating himself. Pride can clothe itself in the garments of praise or of penitence. Even though the words,

"I am not as the rest of men" are rejected and condemned, their spirit may too often be found in our feelings and language towards our fellow worshippers and fellow men. Would you know if this really is so, just listen to the way in which Churches and Christians often speak of one another. How little of the meekness and gentleness of Jesus is to be seen. It is so little remembered that deep humility must be the keynote of what the servants of Jesus say of themselves or each other. Are there not many churches or assemblies of the saints, many missions or conventions, many societies or committees, even many missions away in heathendom, where the harmony has been disturbed and the work of God hindered because men, who are counted saints, have proved in touchiness and haste and impatience, in self-defense and self-assertion, in sharp judgments and unkind words that they did not each reckon others better than themselves, and that their holiness has but little in it of the meekness of the saints?

In their spiritual history men may have had times of great humbling and brokers, but what a different thing this is from being clothed with humility, from having an humble spirit, from having that lowliness of mind in which each counts himself the servant of others, and so shows forth the very mind which was also in Jesus Christ.

"Stand by, for I am holier than thou!" What a parody on holiness! Jesus the Holy One is the humble One; the holiest will ever be the humblest. There is none holy but God; we have as much of holiness as we have of God. And according to what we have of God will be our real humility, because humility is nothing but the disappearance of self in the vision that God is all. The holiest will be the humblest. Alas! though the bare-faced boasting Jew of the days of Isaiah is not often to be found, even our manners have taught us not to speak thus, how often his spirit is still seen, whether in the treatment of fellow saints or of the children of the world. In the spirit in which opinions are given, and work is undertaken, and faults are exposed, how often, though the garb is that of the publican, the voice is still that of the Pharisee: *"God, I thank thee, that I am not as other men are, extortioners, unjust, adulterers, or even as this publican" (Luke 18:11).*

And is there, then, such humility to be found that men shall indeed still count themselves "less than the least of all saints," the servants of all? There is. "Love vaunteth not itself, is not puffed up, seeketh not its own." Where the spirit of love is shed abroad in the heart, where the divine nature comes to a full birth where Christ the meek and lowly Lamb of God is truly formed within, there is given the power of a perfect love that forgets itself and finds its blessedness in blessing others, in bearing with them and honoring them, however feeble they are. Where this love enters, there God enters. And where God has entered in His power, and reveals Himself as All, there the creature becomes nothing.

And where the creature becomes nothing before God; it cannot be anything but humble towards the fellow-creature. The presence of God becomes not a thing of times and seasons, but the covering under which the soul ever dwells, and its deep abasement before God becomes the holy place of His presence whence all its words and works proceed.

May God teach us that our thoughts and words and feelings concerning our fellow men are His test of our humility towards Him, and that our humility before Him is the only power that can enable us to be always humble with our fellow men. Our humility must be the life of Christ, the Lamb of God, within us.

Let all teachers of holiness, whether in the pulpit or on the platform, and all seekers after holiness, whether in the closet or the convention, take warning. There is no pride so dangerous, because none so subtle and insidious, as the pride of holiness. It is not that a man ever says or even thinks, "Stand by; I am holier than thou." No, indeed, the thought would be regarded with abhorrence. But there grows up, all unconsciously, a hidden habit of soul, which feels complacency its attainments, and cannot help seeing how far it is in advance of others. It can be recognized, not always in any special self-assertion or self-laudation, but simply in the absence of that deep self-abasement which cannot but be the mark of the soul that has seen the glory of God (Job 42:5-6; Isaiah 6:5). It reveals itself not only in words or thoughts, but in a tone, a way of speaking of others, in which those who have the gift of spiritual discernment cannot but recognize the power of self. Even the world with its keen eyes notices it, and points to it as a proof that the profession of a heavenly life does not bear any especially heavenly fruits.

O brethren! let us beware. Unless we make, with each advance in what we think holiness, the increase of humility our study, we may find that we have been delighting in beautiful thoughts and feelings, in solemn acts of consecration and faith, while the only sure mark of the presence of God, the disappearance of self, was all the time wanting. Come and let us flee to Jesus, and hide ourselves in Him until we are clothed upon with His humility. That alone is our holiness.

45

CHAPTER 8

Humility and Sin

*This is a faithful saying, and worthy of all
acceptation, that Christ Jesus came into the world
to save sinners; of whom I am chief
(1 Timothy 1:15).*

Humility is often identified with penitence and
contrition. As a consequence, there appears to
be no way of fostering humility except by keeping
the soul occupied with its sin. We have learned, I think,
that humility is something else and something more. We
have seen in the teaching of our Lord Jesus and the Epistles
how often the virtue is inculcated without any reference
to sin. In the very nature of things, in the whole relation of
the creature to the Creator, in the life of Jesus as He lived
it and imparts it to us, humility is the very essence of
holiness as of blessedness. It is the displacement of self by
the enthronement of God. Where God is all, self is nothing.

But though it is this aspect of the truth I have felt it especially needful to press, I scarcely need to say what new depth and intensity man's sin and God's grace give to the humility of the saints. We have only to look at a man like the Apostle Paul to see how, through his life as a ransomed and a holy man, the deep consciousness of having been a sinner lives inextinguishably. We all know the passages in which he refers to his life as a persecutor and blasphemer. *"For I am the least of the apostles, that am not meet to be called an apostle, because I persecuted the church of God. But by the grace of God I am what I am: and his grace which was bestowed upon me was not in vain; but I laboured more abundantly than they all: yet not I, but the grace of God which was with me"* (1 Corinthians 15:9-10). *"Unto me, who am less than the least of all saints, is this grace given, that I should preach among the Gentiles the unsearchable riches of Christ"* (Ephesians 3:8).

"[I] was before a blasphemer, and a persecutor, and injurious; howbeit I obtained mercy, because I did it ignorantly in unbelief ... Christ Jesus came into the world to save sinners, of whom I am chief" (1 Timothy 1:13, 15). God's grace had saved him; God remembered his sins no more for ever; but never, never could he forget how terribly he had sinned. The more he rejoiced in God's salvation, and the more his experience of God's grace filled him with joy unspeakable, the clearer was his consciousness that he was a saved sinner, and that salvation had no meaning or sweetness except as the sense of his being a sinner made it precious and real to him. Never for a moment could he forget that it was a sinner God had taken up in His arms and crowned with His love.

The texts we have just quoted are often appealed to as Paul's confession of daily sinning. One has only to read them carefully in their connection to see how little this is the case. They have a far deeper meaning: they refer to that which lasts throughout eternity, and which will give its deep undertone of amazement and adoration to the humility with which the ransomed bow before the throne, as those who have been washed from their sins in the blood of the Lamb. Never, never, even in glory can they be other than ransomed sinners; never for a moment in this life can God's child live in the full light of His love, but as he feels that the sin, out of which he has been saved, is his one only right and title to all that grace has promised to do. The humility, with which first he came as a sinner, acquires a new meaning when he learns how it becomes him as a creature. And then ever again, the humility, in which he was born as a creature, has its deepest, richest tones of adoration, in the memory of what it is to be a monument of God's wondrous redeeming love.

The true import of what these expressions of St. Paul teach us comes out all the more strongly when we notice the remarkable fact that through his whole Christian course, we never find from his pen, even in those epistles in which we have the most intensely personal unbosomings, anything like confession of sin. Nowhere is there any mention of shortcoming or defect, nowhere any suggestion to his readers that he has failed in duty or sinned against the law of perfect love. On the contrary, there are passages not a few in which he vindicates himself in language that means nothing if it does not appeal to a faultless life before God and men.

"Ye are witnesses, and God also, how holily and justly and unblameably we behaved ourselves among you that believe" (1 Thessalonians 2:10).

"For our rejoicing is this, the testimony of our conscience, that in simplicity and godly sincerity, not with fleshly wisdom, but by the grace of God, we have had our conversation in the world, and more abundantly to you-ward" (2 Corinthians 1:12).

This is not an ideal or an aspiration; it is an appeal to what his actual life had been. However we may account for this absence of confession of sin, all will admit that it must point to a life in the power of the Holy Ghost, such as is, but seldom realized or expected in these our days.

The point which I wish to emphasize is this: that the very fact of the absence of such confession of sinning only gives the more force to the truth that it is not in daily sinning that the secret of the deeper humility will be found, but in the habitual, never for a moment to be forgotten position, which just the more abundant grace will keep more distinctly alive, that our only place, the only place of blessing, our one abiding position before God, must be that of those whose highest joy it is to confess that they are sinners saved by grace.

With Paul's deep remembrance of having sinned so terribly in the past, ere grace had met him, and the consciousness of being kept from present sinning, there was ever coupled the abiding remembrance of the dark hidden power of sin ever ready to come in, and only kept out by the presence and power of the indwelling Christ. *"For I know that in me (that is, in my flesh,) dwelleth no good thing: for to will is present with me; but how to perform that which is good I find not" (Romans 7:18).* These words of Romans 7 describe the flesh as it is to the end. The glorious deliverance of Romans 8. *"For the law of the Spirit of life in Christ Jesus hath made me free from the law of sin and death" (Romans 8:2)* is neither the annihilation nor the sanctification of the flesh, but a continuous victory given by the Spirit as He mortifies the deeds of the body. As health expels disease, and light swallows up darkness, and life conquers death, the indwelling of Christ through the Spirit is the health and light and life of the soul. But with this, the conviction of helplessness and danger ever tempers the faith in the momentary and unbroken action of the Holy Spirit into that chastened sense of dependence which makes the highest faith and joy the handmaids of a humility that only lives by the grace of God.

The three passages above quoted all show that it was the wonderful grace bestowed upon Paul, and of which he felt the need every moment, that humbled him so deeply. The grace of God that was with him, and enabled him to labor more abundantly than they all; the grace to preach to the heathen the unsearchable riches of Christ; the grace that was exceeding abundant with faith and love which is in Christ Jesus, it was this grace of which it is the very nature and glory that it is for sinners, that kept the consciousness of his having once sinned, and being liable to sin, so intensely alive. *"But where sin abounded, grace did much more abound" (Romans 5:20).* This reveals how the very essence of grace is to deal with and take away sin, and how it must ever be the more abundant the experience of grace, the more intense the consciousness of being a sinner. It is not sin, but God's grace showing a man and

51

ever reminding him what a sinner he was, that will keep him truly humble. It is not sin, but grace, that will make me indeed know myself a sinner, and make the sinner's place of deepest self-abasement the place I never leave.

I fear that there are not a few who, by strong expressions of self-condemnation and self-denunciation, have sought to humble themselves, and have to confess with sorrow that a humble spirit, a "heart of humility," with its accompaniments of kindness and compassion, of meekness and forbearance, is still as far off as ever. Being occupied with self, even amid the deepest self-abhorrence, can never free us from self. It is the revelation of God, not only by the law condemning sin, but also by His grace delivering from it that will make us humble. The law may break the heart with fear; it is only grace that works that sweet humility which becomes a joy to the soul as its second nature. It was the revelation of God in His holiness, drawing nigh to make Himself known in His grace, that made Abraham and Jacob, Job and Isaiah, bow so low. It is the soul in which God the Creator, as the All of the creature in its nothingness, God the Redeemer in His grace, as the All of the sinner in his sinfulness, is waited for and trusted and worshipped, that will find itself so filled with His presence, that there will be no place for self. So alone can the promise be fulfilled: "The haughtiness of man shall be brought low, and the Lord alone be exalted in that day."

It is the sinner dwelling in the full light of God's holy, redeeming love, in the experience of that full indwelling of divine love, which comes through Christ and the Holy Spirit, who cannot but be humble. Not to be occupied with thy sin, but to be occupied with God, brings deliverance from self.

CHAPTER 9

Humility and Faith

*How can ye believe, which receive honour one of
another, and seek not the honour that cometh from
God only? (John 5:44)*

$\mathcal{I}$n an address I lately heard, the speaker said that
the blessings of the higher Christian life were often
like the objects exposed in a shop window, one could
see them clearly and yet could not reach them. If told to
stretch out his hand and take, a man would answer, I
cannot; there is a thick pane of glass between them and
me. And even so Christians may see clearly the blessed
promises of perfect peace and rest, of overflowing love
and joy, of abiding communion and fruitfulness, and yet
feel that there was something between hindering the true
possession. And what might that be? Nothing but pride.

The promises made to faith are so free and sure; the
invitations and encouragements so strong; the mighty
power of God on which it may count is so near and free,

that it can only be something that hinders faith that hinders the blessing being ours. In our text Jesus discovers to us that it is indeed pride that makes faith impossible. "How can ye believe, which receive glory from one another?" As we see how in their very nature pride and faith are irreconcilably at variance, we shall learn that faith and humility are at root one, and that we never can have more of true faith than we have of true humility; we shall see that we may indeed have strong intellectual conviction and assurance of the truth while pride is kept in the heart, but that it makes the living faith, which has power with God, an impossibility.

We need only think for a moment what faith is. Is it not the confession of nothingness and helplessness, the surrender and the waiting to let God work? Is it not in itself the most humbling thing there can be, the acceptance of our place as dependents, who can claim or get or do nothing but what grace bestows? Humility is simply the disposition which prepares the soul for living on trust. And every, even the most secret breathing of pride, in self-seeking, self-will, self-confidence, or self-exaltation, is just the strengthening of that self which cannot enter the kingdom, or possess the things of the kingdom, because it refuses to allow God to be what He is and must be there— the All in All.

Faith is the organ or sense for the perception and apprehension of the heavenly world and its blessings. Faith seeks the glory that comes from God, that only comes where God is All. As long as we take glory from one another, as long as ever we seek and love and jealously guard the glory of this life—the honor and reputation that comes from men—we do not seek and cannot receive the glory that comes from God. Pride renders faith impossible. Salvation comes through a cross and a crucified Christ. Salvation is the fellowship with the crucified Christ in the Spirit of His cross. Salvation is union with and delight in, salvation is participation in, the humility of Jesus. Is it any wonder that our faith is so feeble when pride still reigns so much, and we have scarce learnt even to long or pray for humility as the most needful and blessed part of salvation?

Humility and faith are more nearly allied in Scripture than many know. See it in the life of Christ. There are two cases in which He spoke of a great faith. He marveled at the faith of the centurion who said, *"... Lord, I am not worthy that thou shouldest come under my roof ..."* *(Matthew 8:8)*. Christ replied, *"Verily I say unto you, I have not found so great faith, no, not in Israel" (Matthew 8:10)*.

Then there was the mother who accepted the name of dog and said, *"Truth, Lord: yet the dogs eat of the crumbs which fall from their masters' table" (Matthew 15:27)*. And Christ replied, *"O woman, great is thy faith ..."* *(Matthew 15:28)*. It is humility that brings a soul to be nothing before God, removes every hindrance to faith, and makes it only fear lest it should dishonor Him by not trusting Him wholly.

Brother, have we not here the cause of failure in the pursuit of holiness? Is it not this, though we knew it not, that made our consecration and our faith so superficial and so short-lived? We had no idea to what an extent pride and self were still secretly working within us, and how God alone by His incoming and His mighty power could cast them out. We understood not how the new and divine nature, alone and taking entirely the place of the old self, could make us really humble. We knew not that absolute, unceasing, universal humility must be the root disposition of every prayer and every approach to God as well as of every dealing with man; and that we might as well attempt to see without eyes or live without breath, as believe or draw nigh to God or dwell in His love without an all-pervading humility and lowliness of heart.

Brother, have we not been making a mistake in taking so much trouble to believe, while all the time there was the old self in its pride seeking to possess itself of God's blessing and riches? No wonder we could not believe. Let us change our course. Let us seek first of all to humble ourselves under the mighty hand of God. He will exalt us. The cross, and the death, and the grave into which Jesus humbled Himself were His path to the glory of God. And they are our path. Let our one desire and our fervent prayer be to be humbled with Him and like Him; let us accept gladly whatever can humble us before God or men; this alone is the path to the glory of God.

You perhaps feel inclined to ask a question. I have spoken of some who have blessed experiences, or are the means of bringing blessing to others, and yet are lacking in humility. You ask whether or not these do not prove that they have true, even strong faith, though they show too clearly that they still seek too much the honor that cometh from men. More than one answer can be given. But the principal answer in our present connection is this: They indeed have a measure of faith, in proportion to which, with the special gifts bestowed upon them, is the blessing they bring to others. But in that very blessing the work of their faith is hindered through the lack of humility.

The blessing is often superficial or transitory, just because they are not the nothing that opens the way for God to be all. A deeper humility would without doubt bring a deeper and fuller blessing. The Holy Spirit, working in them as a Spirit of power, and dwelling in them in the fullness of His grace, and specially that of humility, would through them communicate Himself to these converts for a life of power and holiness and steadfastness now all too little seen.

"How can ye believe, which receive glory from one another?" Brother! nothing can cure you of the desire of receiving glory from men, or of the sensitiveness and pain and anger which come when it is not given, but giving yourself to seek only the glory that comes from God. Let the glory of the All glorious God be everything to you. You will be freed from the glory of men and of self, and be content and glad to be nothing. Out of this nothingness you will grow strong in faith, giving glory to God, and you will find that the deeper you sink in humility before Him, the nearer He is to fulfill the every desire of your faith.

CHAPTER 10

Humility and Death to Self

And being found in fashion as a man, he humbled himself, and became obedient unto death, even the death of the cross (Philippians 2:8).

*H*umility is the path to death, because in death humililty gives the highest proof of its perfection. Humility is the blossom of which death to self is the perfect fruit. Jesus humbled Himself unto death, and opened the path in which we too must walk. As there was no way for Him to prove His surrender to God to the very uttermost, or to give up and rise out of our human nature to the glory of the Father but through death, so with us, too. Humility must lead us to die to self: so we prove how wholly we have given ourselves up to it and to God; so alone we are freed from fallen nature, and find the path that leads to life in God, to that full birth of the new nature, of which humility is the breath and the joy.

We have spoken of that which Jesus did for His disciples when He communicated His resurrection life to them, when in the descent of the Holy Spirit, He, the glorified and enthroned Meekness, actually came from heaven Himself to dwell in them. He won the power to do this through death. In its inmost nature, the life He imparted was a life out of death, a life that had been surrendered to death and been won through death. He who came to dwell in them was Himself One who had been dead and now lives for evermore. His life, His person, His presence bear the marks of death, of being a life begotten out of death. That life in His disciples ever bears the deathmarks, too. It is only as the Spirit of the death, of the dying One, dwells and works in the soul, that the power of His life can be known. The first and chief of the marks of the dying of the Lord Jesus, of the death-marks that show the true follower of Jesus, is humility. For these two reasons: Only humility leads to perfect death; only death perfects humility. Humility and death are in their very nature one: humility is the bud; in death the fruit is ripened to perfection.

Humility leads to perfect death. Humility means the giving up of self and the taking of the place of perfect nothingness before God. Jesus humbled Himself, and became obedient unto death. In death He gave the highest, the perfect proof of having given up His will to the will of God. In death He gave up His self, with its natural reluctance to drink the cup. He gave up the life He had in union with our human nature. He died to self, and the sin that tempted Him; so, as man, He entered into the perfect life of God. If it had not been for His boundless humility, counting Himself as nothing except as a servant to do and suffer the will of God, He never would have died.

This gives us the answer to the question so often asked and of which the meaning is so seldom clearly apprehended: How can I die to self? The death to self is not your work; it is God's work. In Christ you are dead to sin. The life there is in you has gone through the process of death and resurrection; you may be sure you are indeed dead to sin. But the full manifestation of the power of this death in your disposition and conduct depends upon the measure in which the Holy Spirit imparts the power of the death of Christ. And here it is that the teaching is needed: if you would enter into full fellowship with Christ in His death and know the full deliverance from self, humble yourself. This is your one duty.

Place yourself before God in your utter helplessness; consent heartily to the fact of your impotence to slay or make alive yourself. Sink down into your own nothingness, in the spirit of meek and patient and trustful surrender to God. Accept every humiliation. Look upon every fellow man who tries or vexes you as a means of grace to humble you. Use every opportunity of humbling yourself before your fellow men as a help to abide humbly before God. God will accept such humbling of yourself as the proof that your whole heart desires it, as the very best prayer for it, as your preparation for His mighty work of grace, when, by the mighty strengthening of His Holy Spirit, He reveals Christ fully in you, so that He, in His form of a servant, is truly formed in you, and dwells in your heart. It is the path of humility that leads to perfect death, the full and perfect experience that we are dead in Christ.

Then follows: Only this death leads to perfect humility. Oh, beware of the mistake so many make, who would fain be humble, but are afraid to be too humble. They have so many qualifications and limitations, so many reasonings and questionings, as to what true humility is to be and to do, that they never unreservedly yield themselves to it. Beware of this.

Humble yourself unto the death. It is in the death to self that humility is perfected. Be sure that at the root of all real experience of more grace, of all true advance in consecration, of all actually increasing conformity to the likeness of Jesus, there must be a deadness to self that proves itself to God and men in our dispositions and habits. It is sadly possible to speak of the death-life and the Spirit-walk, while even the tenderest love cannot but see how much there is of self. The death to self has no surer deathmark than a humility that makes itself of no reputation, which empties out itself, and takes the form of a servant. It is possible to speak much and honestly of fellowship with a despised and rejected Jesus, and of bearing His cross, while the meek and lowly, the kind and gentle humility of the Lamb of God is not seen and is scarcely sought. The Lamb of God means two things: meekness and death. Let us seek to receive Him in both forms. In Him they are inseparable. They must be in us, too.

What a hopeless task if we had to do the work! Nature never can overcome nature, not even with the help of grace. Self can never cast out self, even in the regenerate man. Praise God! The work has been done and finished and perfected forever. The death of Jesus, once and for ever, is our death to self. And the ascension of Jesus, His entering once and for ever into the Holiest, has given us the Holy Spirit to communicate to us in power, and make our very own, the power of the death-life. As the soul, in the pursuit and practice of humility, follows in the steps of Jesus, its consciousness of the need of something more is awakened; its desire and hope is quickened; its faith is strengthened; and it learns to look up and claim and receive that true fullness of the Spirit of Jesus, which can daily maintain His death to self and sin in its full power, and make humility the all pervading spirit of our life. (See note at end of this chapter.)

"Know ye not, that so many of us as were baptized into Jesus Christ were baptized into his death? ... Likewise reckon ye also yourselves to be dead indeed unto sin, but alive unto God through Jesus Christ our Lord" (Romans 6:3, 11).

The whole self-consciousness of the Christian is to be imbued and characterized by the spirit that animated the death of Christ. He has ever to present himself to God as one who has died in Christ, and in Christ is alive from the dead, bearing about in his body the dying of the Lord Jesus. His life ever bears the two-fold mark: its roots striking in true humility deep into the grave of Jesus, the death to sin and self; its head lifted up in resurrection power to the heaven where Jesus is.

Believer, claim in faith the death and the life of Jesus as thine. Enter in His grave into the rest from self and its work the rest of God. With Christ, who committed His spirit into the Father's hands, humble thyself and descend each day into that perfect, helpless dependence upon God. God will raise thee up and exalt thee. Sink every morning in deep, deep nothingness into the grave of Jesus; every day the life of Jesus will be manifest in thee. Let a willing, loving, restful, happy humility be the mark that thou hast indeed claimed thy birthright—the baptism into the death of Christ. "By one offering He has perfected for ever them that are sanctified." The souls that enter into His humiliation will find in Him the power to see and count self dead, and, as those who have learned and received of Him, to walk with all lowliness and meekness, forbearing one another in love. The death-life is seen in a meekness and lowliness like that of Christ.

Chapter Endnote

To die to self, or come from under its power, is not, cannot be done by any active resistance we can make to it by the powers of nature. The one true way of dying to self is the way of patience, meekness, humility, and resignation to God. This is the truth and perfection of dying to self ... For if I ask you what the Lamb of God means, must you not tell me that it is and means the perfection of patience, meekness, humility, and resignation to God? Must you not therefore say that a desire and faith of these virtues is an application to Christ, is a giving up yourself to Him and the perfection of faith in Him? And then, because this inclination of your heart to sink down in patience, meekness, humility, and resignation to God is truly giving up all that you are and all that you have from fallen Adam, it is perfectly leaving all you have to follow Christ. It is your highest act of faith in Him. Christ is nowhere but in these virtues; when they are there, He is in His own kingdom. Let this be the Christ you follow.

The Spirit of divine love can have no birth in any fallen creature, till it wills and chooses to be dead to all self in patient, humble resignation to the power and mercy of

God. I seek for all my salvation through the merits and mediation of the meek, humble, patient, suffering Lamb of God, who alone hath power to bring forth the blessed birth of these heavenly virtues in my soul. There is no possibility of salvation except in and by the birth of the meek, humble, patient, resigned Lamb of God in our souls. When the Lamb of God hath brought forth a real birth of His own meekness, humility, and full resignation to God in our souls, then it is the birthday of the Spirit of love in our souls, which, whenever we attain, will feast our souls with such peace and joy in God as will blot out the remembrance of everything that we called peace or joy before.

This way to God is infallible. This infallibility is grounded in the twofold character of our Savior: 1. As He is the Lamb of God, a principal of all meekness and humility in the soul.

2. As He is the Light of heaven and blesses eternal nature and turns it into a kingdom of heaven, when we are willing to get rest to our souls in meek, humble resignation to God, then it is that He, as the Light of God and heaven, joyfully breaks in upon us, turns our darkness into light, and begins that kingdom of God and of love within us, which will never have an end.

CHAPTER 11

Humility and Happiness

Most gladly therefore will I rather glory in my infirmities, that the power of Christ may rest upon me. Therefore I take pleasure in infirmities, in reproaches, in necessities, in persecutions, in distresses for Christ's sake: for when I am weak, then am I strong (2 Corinthians 12:9-10).

Lest Paul should exalt himself, by reason of the exceeding greatness of the revelations, a thorn in the flesh was sent him to keep him humble. Paul's first desire was to have it removed, and he besought the Lord thrice that it might depart. The answer came that the trial was a blessing; that, in the weakness and humiliation it brought, the grace and strength of the Lord could be the better manifested. Paul at once entered upon a new stage in his relation to the trial: instead of simply enduring it, he most gladly gloried in it. Instead of asking for deliverance, he took pleasure in it. He had learnt that the place of humiliation is the place of blessing, of power, of joy.

Every Christian virtually passes through these two stages in his pursuit of humility. In the first he fears and flees and seeks deliverance from all that can humble him. He has not yet learnt to seek humility at any cost. He has accepted the command to be humble, and seeks to obey it, though only to find how utterly he fails. He prays for humility, at times very earnestly; but in his secret heart he prays more, if not in word, then in wish, to be kept from the very things that will make him humble. He is not yet so in love with humility as the beauty of the Lamb of God, and the joy of heaven, that he would sell all to procure it. In his pursuit of it and his prayer for it, there is still somewhat of a sense of burden and of bondage. To humble himself has not yet become the spontaneous expression of a life and a nature that is essentially humble. It has not yet become his joy and only pleasure. He cannot yet say, "Most gladly do I glory in weakness, I take pleasure in whatever humbles me."

But can we hope to reach the stage in which this will be the case? Undoubtedly. And what will it be that brings us there? That which brought Paul there—a new revelation of the Lord Jesus. Nothing but the presence of God can reveal and expel self. A clearer insight was to be given to Paul into the deep truth that the presence of Jesus will banish every desire to seek anything in ourselves, and will make us delight in every humiliation that prepares us for His fuller manifestation. Our humiliations lead us, in the experience of the presence and power of Jesus, to choose humility as our highest blessing. Let us try to learn the lessons the story of Paul teaches us.

We may have advanced believers, eminent teachers, men of heavenly experiences, who have not yet fully learnt the lesson of perfect humility, gladly glorying in weakness. We see this in Paul. The danger of exalting himself was coming very near. He knew not yet perfectly what it was to be nothing and to die, that Christ alone might live in him, to take pleasure in all that brought him low. It appears as if this were the highest lesson that he had to learn, full conformity to his Lord in that self-emptying where he gloried in weakness that God might be all.

The highest lesson a believer has to learn is humility. Oh that every Christian who seeks to advance in holiness may remember this well! There may be intense consecration and fervent zeal and heavenly experience, and yet, if it is not prevented by very special dealings of the Lord, there may be an unconscious self-exaltation with it all. Let us learn the lesson: the highest holiness is the deepest humility. Let us remember that comes not of itself, but only as it is made a matter of special dealing on the part of our faithful Lord and His faithful servant.

Let us look at our lives in the light of this experience, and see whether we gladly glory in weakness, whether we take pleasure, as Paul did, in injuries, in necessities, in distresses. Yes, let us ask whether we have learnt to regard a reproof—just or unjust—a reproach from friend or enemy, an injury or trouble or difficulty into which others bring us, as, above all, an opportunity of proving Jesus is all to us, how our own pleasure or honor are nothing, and how humiliation is, in very truth, that in which we take pleasure. It is indeed blessed, the deep happiness of heaven, to be so free from self that whatever is said of us or done to us is lost and swallowed up, in the thought that Jesus is all.

Let us trust Him who took charge of Paul to take charge of us, too. Paul needed special discipline, and, with it, special instruction to learn what was more precious than even the unutterable things he had heard in heaven, what it is to glory in weakness and lowliness. We need it, too, oh so much. He who cared for him will care for us, too. He watches over us with a jealous, loving care, "lest we exalt ourselves." When we are doing so, He seeks to discover to us the evil and deliver us from it. In trial and weakness and trouble He seeks to bring us low until we learn that His grace is all, and take pleasure in the very thing that brings us and keeps us low. His strength made perfect in our weakness and His presence filling and satisfying our emptiness become the secret of a humility that need never fail. It can, as Paul, in full sight of what God works in us and through us, ever say, "In nothing was I behind the chiefest apostles, though I am nothing." His humiliations had led him to true humility with its wonderful gladness and glorying and pleasure in all that humbles.

"Most gladly therefore will I rather glory in my infirmities, that the power of Christ may rest upon me" *(2 Corinthians 12:9).* The humble man has learnt the secret of abiding gladness. The weaker he feels, the lower he sinks, the greater his humiliations appear, the more the power and the presence of Christ are his portion, until, as he says, "I am nothing," the word of his Lord brings ever deeper joy: "My grace is sufficient for thee."

I feel as if I must once again gather up all in the two lessons: the danger of pride is greater and nearer than we think, and the grace for humility, too.

The danger of pride is greater and nearer than we think, and that especially at the time of our highest experiences. The preacher of spiritual truth with an admiring congregation hanging on his lips, the gifted speaker on a Holiness platform expounding the secrets of the heavenly life, the Christian giving testimony to a blessed experience, the evangelist moving on as in triumph and made a blessing to rejoicing multitudes, no man knows the hidden, unconscious danger to which these are exposed. Paul was in danger without knowing it; what Jesus did for him is written for our admonition, that we may know our danger and know our only safety. If ever it has been said of a teacher or professor of holiness, he is so full of self; or, he does not practice what he preaches; or, his blessing has not made him humbler or gentler, let it be said no more. Jesus, in whom we trust, can make us humble.

Yes, the grace for humility is greater and nearer, too, than we think. The humility of Jesus is our salvation: Jesus Himself is our humility. Our humility is His care and His work. His grace is sufficient for us, to meet the temptation of pride, too. His strength will be perfected in our weakness. Let us choose to be weak, to be low, to be nothing. Let humility be to us joy and gladness. Let us gladly glory and take pleasure in weakness, in all that can humble us and keep us low; the power of Christ will rest upon us. Christ humbled Himself; therefore God exalted Him. Christ will humble us, and keep us humble; let us heartily consent. Let us trustfully and joyfully accept all that humbles. The power of Christ will rest upon us. We shall find that the deepest humility is the secret of the truest happiness, of a joy that nothing can destroy.

CHAPTER 12

Humility and Exaltation

For whosoever exalteth himself shall be abased;
and he that humbleth himself shall be exalted
(Luke 14:11).

Humble yourselves in the sight of the Lord,
and he shall lift you up (James 4:10).

Humble yourselves therefore under the mighty hand
of God, that he may exalt you in due time
(1 Peter 5:6).

*J*ust yesterday I was asked the question, How am I to conquer this pride? The answer was simple. Two things are needed. Do that which God says is your work and humble yourself. Trust Him to do what He says is His work; He will exalt you.

The command is clear: humble yourself. That does not mean that it is your work to conquer and cast out the pride of your nature, and to form within yourself the lowliness of the holy Jesus. No, this is God's work: the very essence of that exaltation, wherein He lifts you up into the real likeness of the beloved Son. What the command does mean is this: take every opportunity of humbling yourself before God and man. In the faith of the grace that is already working in you, in the assurance of the more grace for victory that is coming, up to the light that conscience each time flashes upon the pride of the heart and its workings, notwithstanding all there may be of failure and falling, stand persistently as under the unchanging command: humble yourself.

Accept with gratitude everything that God allows from within or without, from friend or enemy, in nature or in grace, to remind you of your need of humbling, and to help you to it. Reckon humility to be indeed the mother-virtue, your very first duty before God, the one perpetual safeguard of the soul; and set your heart upon it as the source of all blessing. The promise is divine and sure: He that humbleth himself shall be exalted. See that you do the one thing God asks: humble yourself. God will do the one thing He has promised. He will give more grace. He will exalt you in due time.

All God's dealings with man are characterized by two stages. There is the time of preparation, when command and promise, with the mingled experience of effort and impotence, of failure and partial success, with the holy expectancy of something better which these waken, train and discipline men for a higher stage. Then comes the time of fulfillment, when faith inherits the promise and enjoys what it had so often struggled for in vain. This law holds good in every part of the Christian life, and in the pursuit of every separate virtue. It is grounded in the very nature of things. In all that concerns our redemption, God must take the initiative. When that has been done, man's turn comes. In the effort after obedience and attainment, he must learn to know his impotence, in self-despair to die to himself, and so be fitted voluntarily and intelligently to receive from God the end, the completion of that which he had accepted the beginning in ignorance. So, God who had been the Beginning, ere man rightly knew Him, or fully understood what His purpose was, is longed for and welcomed as the End, as the All in All.

It is even thus, too, in the pursuit of humility. To every Christian the command comes from the throne of God Himself: humble yourself. The earnest attempt to listen and obey will be rewarded, yes, rewarded with the painful discovery of two things. The one, what depth of pride, that is of unwillingness to count oneself and to be counted nothing, to submit absolutely to God, there was, that one never knew. The other, what utter impotence there is in all our efforts and in all our prayers, too, for God's help, to destroy the hideous monster. Blessed the man who now learns to put his hope in God and to persevere, notwithstanding all the power of pride within him, in acts of humiliation before God and men. We know the law of human nature: acts produce habits, habits breed dispositions, dispositions form the will, and the rightly formed will is character. It is not otherwise in the work of grace. As acts, persistently repeated, beget habits and dispositions, and these strengthened the will, He who works both to will and to do comes with His mighty power and Spirit; and the humbling of the proud heart with which the penitent saint casts himself so often before God, is rewarded with the "more grace" of the humble heart, in which the Spirit of Jesus has conquered, and brought the new nature to its maturity, and He, the meek and lowly One, now dwells for ever.

Humble yourselves in the sight of the Lord, and He will exalt you. And wherein does the exaltation consist? The highest glory of the creature is in being only a vessel to receive and enjoy and show forth the glory of God. It can do this only as it is willing to be nothing in itself, that God may be all. Water always fills first the lowest places. The lower, the emptier a man lies before God, the speedier and the fuller will be the inflow of the divine glory. The exaltation God promises is not, cannot be any external thing apart from Himself. All that He has to give or can give is only more of Himself, Himself to take more complete possession. The exaltation is not, like an earthly prize, something arbitrary, in no necessary connection with the conduct to be rewarded. No, but it is in its very nature the effect and result of the humbling of ourselves. It is nothing but the gift of such a divine indwelling humility, such a conformity to and possession of the humility of the Lamb of God, as fits us for receiving fully the indwelling of God.

He that humbleth himself shall be exalted. Of the truth of these words, Jesus Himself is the proof. Of the certainty of their fulfillment to us, He is the pledge. Let us take His yoke upon us and learn of Him, for He is meek and lowly of heart. If we are but willing to stoop to Him, as He has stooped to us, He will yet stoop to each one of us again, and we shall find ourselves not unequally yoked with Him. As we enter deeper into the fellowship of His humiliation, and either humble ourselves or bear the humbling of men, we can count upon it that the Spirit of His exaltation, "the Spirit of God and of glory," will rest upon us. The presence and the power of the glorified Christ will come to them that are of an humble spirit. When God can again have His rightful place in us, He will lift us up. Make His glory thy care in humbling thyself; He will make thy glory His care in perfecting thy humility, and breathing into thee, as thy abiding life, the very Spirit of His Son. As the all-pervading life of God possesses thee, there will be nothing so natural and nothing so sweet as to be nothing with not a thought or wish for self, because all is occupied with Him who filleth all. "Most gladly will I glory in my weakness, that the strength of Christ may rest upon me."

Brother, have we not here the reason that our consecration and our faith have availed so little in the pursuit of holiness? It was by self and its strength that the work was done under the name of faith. It was for self and its happiness that God was called in. It was, unconsciously, but still truly in self and its holiness that the soul rejoiced. We never knew that humility, absolute, abiding, Christ-like humility and self-effacement, pervading and marking our whole life with God and man, was the most essential element of the life of the holiness we sought for.

It is only in the possession of God that I lose myself. As it is in the height and breadth and glory of the sunshine that the littleness of the mote playing in its beams is seen, even so humility is the taking our place in God's presence to be nothing but a mote dwelling in the sunlight of His love.

"How great is God! How small am I! Lost, swallowed up in Love's immensity! God only there, not I."

May God teach us to believe that to be humble, to be nothing in His presence is the highest attainment and the fullest blessing of the Christian life. He speaks to us: "I dwell in the high and holy place, and with him who is of a contrite and humble spirit." Be this our portion!

> "Oh, to be emptier, lowlier,
> Mean, unnoticed, and unknown,
> And to God a vessel holier,
> Filled with Christ, and Christ alone!"

Chapter Endnote

Till the spirit of the heart is renewed, till it is emptied of all earthly desires and stands in an habitual hunger and thirst after God, which is the true spirit of prayer; till then, all our prayer will be, more or less, but too much like lessons given to scholars; and we shall mostly say them, only because we dare not neglect them. But be not discouraged; take the following advice, and then you may go to church without any danger of mere lip-labor or hypocrisy, although there should be a hymn or a prayer, whose language is higher than that of your heart.

Do this: go to the church as the publican went to the temple. Stand inwardly in the spirit of your mind in that form which he outwardly expressed, when he cast down his eyes, and could only say, "God be merciful to me, a sinner." Stand unchangeably, at least in your desire, in this form or state of heart; it will sanctify every petition that comes out of your mouth. When anything is read or sung or prayed that is more exalted than your heart is, if you make this an occasion of further sinking down in the spirit of the publican, you will then be helped and highly blessed by those prayers and praises which seem only to belong to a heart better than yours.

This, my friend, is a secret of secrets. It will help you to reap where you have not sown, and be a continual source of grace in your soul; for everything that inwardly stirs in you or outwardly happens to you becomes a real good to you, if it finds or excites in you this humble state of mind. For nothing is in vain or without profit to the humble soul; it stands always in a state of divine growth. Everything that falls upon it is like a dew of heaven to it.

Shut up yourself, therefore, in this form of humility; all good is enclosed in it. It is a water of heaven that turns the fire of the fallen soul into the meekness of the divine life and creates that oil, out of which the love to God and man gets its flame. Be enclosed, therefore, always in it. Let it be as a garment wherewith you are always covered, and a girdle with which you are girt. Breathe nothing but in and from its spirit. See nothing but with its eyes. Hear nothing but with its ears. And then, whether you are in the church or out of the church, hearing the praises of God or receiving wrongs from men and the world, all will be edification, and everything will help forward your growth in the life of God.

[Editor's Note: Murray referred to this endnote as "A Secret of Secrets: Humility as the Soul of True Prayer."]

A Prayer for Humility

I will here give you an infallible touchstone that will try all to the truth. It is this: retire from the world and all conversation only for one month; neither write, nor read, nor debate anything with yourself; stop all the former workings of your heart and mind; and, with all the strength of your heart, stand all this month, as continually as you can, in the following form of prayer to God. Offer it frequently on your knees; but whether sitting, walking, or standing, be always inwardly longing, and earnestly praying this one prayer to God:

"That of Your great goodness You would make known to me, and take from my heart every kind and form and degree of Pride, whether it be from evil spirits or my own corrupt nature; and that You would awaken in me the deepest depth and truth of that Humility, which can make me capable of Your light and Holy Spirit."

Reject every thought, but that of waiting and praying in this matter from the bottom of your heart with such truth and earnestness, as people in torment wish to pray and be delivered from it ... If you can and will give yourself up in truth and sincerity to this spirit of prayer, I will venture to affirm that if you have twice as many evil spirits in you as Mary Magdalene had, they will all be cast out of you, and you will be forced with her to weep tears of love at the feet of the holy Jesus. (*The Spirit of Prayer*, Pt. II, p. 124)

Index

Pure Gold Classics

BEST-SELLING COLLECTIBLES IN AN EXPANDING SERIES

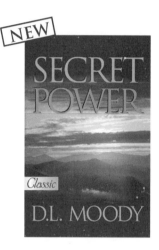

NEW

- Timeline
- Indexes
- Biographies
- Illustrated
- Bible Study
- Collectible
- Modern English

7 Point Advantage

IF YOU ENJOYED
THIS BOOK,
CONSIDER THESE
TITLES FROM
BRIDGE-LOGOS

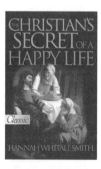

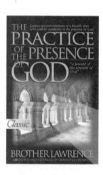

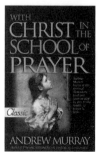

SENSITIVELY REVISED IN MODERN ENGLISH

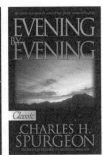

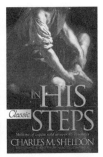

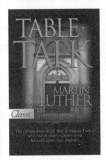

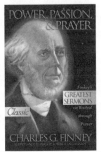

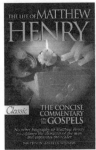

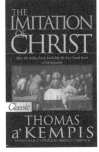

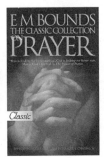

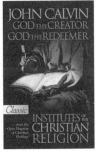

AVAILABLE AT FINE CHRISTIAN BOOKSTORES

03-1758 Jonathan
...vards great American
...ologian and author,
...luding sermon *Sinners in*
...*Hands of an Angry God.*

14-1770 George
...itefield, Calvinist
...angelist known for
...werful preaching and
...ivals in England and
...erica. Friend of John
...sley.

03-1791 John Wesley,
...nder of modern day
...ethodist church, authors
...any landmark sermons,
...luding *The Holy Spirit*
...*d Power.*

20-1750 "The Great
...akening" in America.
...merous revivals
...ulting in widespread
...urch growth.

41 Handel's *Messiah*
...mposed.

56-1763 Seven Years
...r in Europe, Britain
...eats France.

79 Olney Hymns
...blished, John Newton's
...*azing Grace.*

75-1783 American
...volutionary War

89 French Revolution
...gins.

92-1875 Charles Finney,
...nerican evangelist. Leads
...cond Great Awakening
...1824.

16-1900 J. C. Ryle,
...thor of *Practical Religion*
...d *Holiness.*

20-1915 "Fanny" Crosby,
...ough blind, pens over
...000 hymns.

1828-1917 Andrew
Murray, author of *Humility,
Abide in Christ,* and *With
Christ in the School of
Prayer.*

1828 Noah Webster
publishes a dictionary of
the English Language.

1829 Salvation Army
founded by William and
Catherine Booth.

1832-1911 Hannah Whitall
Smith, pens *The Christian's
Secret to a Happy Life* and
God of All Comfort.

1834-1892 Charles H.
Spurgeon, author of
Morning by Morning and
The Treasury of David.

1835-1941 E.M. Bounds,
author of *The Classic
Collection on Prayer*

1837-1897 Dwight Lyman
Moody, evangelist and
founder of Moody Bible
Institute in Chicago. Author
of *Secret Power* and *The
Way to God.*

1844 Samuel Frank Morse
invents the telegraph.

1857-1858 Third Great
Awakening in America;
Prayer Meeting Revival.

1859 Theory of evolution;
Charles Darwin's *Origin of
Species.*

1851-1897 Henry
Drummond, author of *The
Greatest Thing in the World
… Love.*

1857-1949 Charles
Sheldon, author of *In His
Steps.*

1861-1865 American Civil War

1867 Alexander Graham
Bell invents the telephone.

1869-1948 Mahatma
Gandhi makes his life's work
peaceful independence
from Britain for India.

1898-1900 Boxer
Rebellion in China
deposes western influence,
particularly Christian
missionaries.

1901 American Standard
Version of Bible published.

1906 Azusa Street Revival,
Los Angeles, instrumental
in rise of modern
Pentecostal movement.

1906-1945 Dietrich
Bonhoeffer, spreads
Christian faith to Germans
in opposition to WWII
Nazism.

1914-1918 World War I

1917 Bolshevik Revolution
in Russia

1881-1936 J. Gresham
Machen, "Old School"
Presbyterian leader writes
Christianity and Liberalism;
forms the new Orthodox
Presbyterian Church in 1936.

1925 Scopes Monkey Trial
pits Bible against theory of
evolution.

1929 US Stock Market
crashes, 12 years of Great
Depression.

1939-1945 World War II.
Holocaust in eastern
Europe under Hitler.

1947 Dead Sea Scrolls found
in caves in Judean Desert.

1948 State of Israel
reestablished.

1949 Communist
revolution in China; religion
suppressed.

1952 RSV Bible first
published.

1952 American Jonas Salk
develops vaccine against
polio.

1959 China invades Tibet.

1960s Civil Rights
movement in the United
States.

1960s Post-colonial
independence of many
African and Asian countries.

1969 US astronaut Neil
Armstrong walks on the
moon.

1971 NASB Bible first
published.

1978 Soviets invite
international evangelist,
Billy Graham, Christian
gospel to Communist
people.

1978 NIV Bible first
published.

1989 Berlin Wall comes
down.

1989 NRSV Bible first
published.

1990s World Wide Web
globalizes communication;
new means to disseminate
Gospel message.

1991 Communist
government in Soviet
Union crumbles.

2001 September 11th
terrorist attack on the
United States.

4-6 BC Jesus of Nazareth born

27 Christ crucified and risen.

29 Pentecost

35 Stephen, first Christian martyr

37 Paul's conversion and beginning of missionary work.

47 The term "Christian" first used.

58 Emperor Ming-Ti introduces Buddhism to his country.

64 Fire destroys Rome. Emperor Nero blames the Christians.

66 First Jewish revolt against Rome; Paul of Tarsus and Jesus's brother James martyred.

68-70 Dead Sea Scrolls buried in Qumram caves. Found in 1949.

70 Titus destroys Jerusalem and its Temple. Dispersion of the Jews.

95 Apostle John writes Book of Revelation.

105 Paper invented in China.

150 "The First Apologist," Justin Martyr advances Christian efforts against competing philosophies.

190 First "official" date of Easter.

231 Origen's Polygott Bible.

300 Persecution of Christians under Diocletian.

313 Constantine issues *Edict of Milan*, granting legal rights to all Christians in the Roman Empire.

325 Council of Nicea settles heretical challenges to the doctrine of the deity of Christ by Arius.

367 Athanasius compiles earliest known list of New Testament canon in current form.

387 Augustine of Hippo converts to Christianity, later writes his *Confessions* and *City of God*.

395 Roman Empire divided between East and West, setting stage for division of the Christian Church.

400 Vulgate Latin text becomes standard Bible of Christianity.

410 Fall of Roman Empire to the Visigoths, lead by Alaric.

430 Patrick brings Christianity to pagan Ireland.

450 Bodhidharma founds Zen Buddhism in India; takes to China.

451 Council of Chalcedon affirms apostolic doctrine that Christ is "truly God and truly man."

451 The Romans and Visigoths defeat Atilla the Hun at Chalons.

478 First Shinto religious shrines erected in Japan.

529 Benedictine order establishes rule for monastic life.

542-594 Bubonic Plague cuts population of Europe in half.

622 Birth of Islamic religion

640 Library of Alexandria with 30,000 manuscripts completely destroyed.

732 Battle of Poitiers: Muslim forces defeated in France; kept Islam out of Europe.

800 "By the sword and the Cross" Charlemagne restores social and religious order to medieval Europe.

871-901 King Alfred preserves Christianity amidst opposition within and outside the Church.

988 Vladimir converts; brings Christianity to Russia.

1000 Viking Leif Erickson discovers North America.

1000 Chinese perfect the use and production of gunpowder.

1050 First agricultural revolution of Europe begins.

1054 Permanent separation between the Roman Church in the West and Eastern Orthodox Church.

1066 Norman conquest of England under William fuses French and English cultures. As a result, English language evolves into "Middle English."

1085 Christians conquer Toledo; discover works of Aristotle, Plato.

1090-1153 Bernard of Clairvaux

1096 First of eight Christian Crusades begins in effort to prevail over Muslim Invaders.

1140-1217 Peter Waldo, founder of the Protestant Waldenses.

1182 Magnetic compass invented.

1182-1226 Francis of Assisi

1207 Genghis Khan conquers Asia.

1270 Last Christian Crusade

1280 Eyeglasses are invented.

1298 Marco Polo writes *The Travels of Marco Polo.*

1329-1384 John Wycliff translates Bible into English. It's condemned, and forbidden by Archbishop.

1337-1453 Hundred Years War between France and England.

1342-1400 Chaucer writes the *Canterbury Tales* in 1386.

1347 Black Death kills 25 million and halts economic growth in Europe for 200 years.

CHRISTIAN HISTORY **CLASSIC AUTHORS** SECULAR HISTORY **SECULAR AUTHORS & ARTISTS**

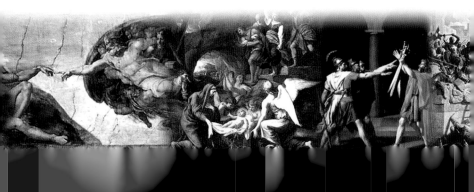

350-1527 Approximate dates of the Renaissance.

369-1415 John Huss, Czech religious reformer before the Reformation. Burned at the stake for his bold stand against corrupt clergy.

368 Chinese Ming Dynasty continues through 644.

378-1417 Great Schism brings competing popes to the Church.

380-1471 Thomas a' Kempis' The Imitation of Christ, published 1427.

386-1466 Donatello, Florentine sculptor who created first freestanding statues in the Renaissance.

420 Huss followers, "Hussites" revolt under John Zizka.

431 Joan of Arc burned at stake.

1450 Johannes Gutenberg invents the printing press.

1452-1519 Leonardo da Vinci, Italian sculptor, architect, painter, inventor, engineer, and scientist.

1453 Fall of Constantinople to the Turks; renamed Istanbul.

1455 Gutenberg Bible printed. Availability and affordability of Bibles becomes a key factor in the ensuing Protestant Reformation.

1469-1527 Niccolo Marchiavelli, Italian philosopher and author of The Prince.

1471-1528 Albrecht Durer, German, Christian artist and sculptor of The Praying Hands.

1473-1543 Nicholaus Copernicus, Polish astronomer founds modern astronomy.

1475-1564 Michelangelo, Florentine sculptor and painter: The Pieta, Moses, David and the Sistine Chapel ceiling.

1477 First book printed in England.

1478 Spanish Inquisition begins.

1483-1546 Martin Luther

1488 The Portuguese round the Cape of Good Hope on southern tip of Africa.

1492 Columbus lands in America.

1497 Italian explorer settles in England, takes the name John Cabot, sails in the name of the Royal Crown and discovers Newfoundland.

1500s Spanish conquer Aztec, Inca civilizations in New World.

1505-1572 John Knox, reformer of Scotland.

1509-1564 John Calvin, French theologian, author. Pens Institutes of Christian Religion in 1536.

1516-1587 John Foxe, author of Book of Martyrs in 1563.

1517 Protestant Reformation begins. Martin Luther posts his 95 Theses against the selling of indulgences.

1525 William Tyndale translates the New Testament from Greek into English. Martyred in 1536.

1533-1584 Ivan the Terrible rules Russia.

1536 King Henry VIII breaks with the Church of Rome.

1545 Council of Trent convenes to refute accusations of heresy made by Protestants. Beginning of Tridentine Church, today's Roman Catholic Church.

1553 Mary "Bloody Mary" Tudor begins her reign.

1555 Leading early reformers Cranmer, Latimer and Ridley burned at stake.

1560 Geneva Bible, the first complete Bible to be translated into English from Hebrew and Greek.

1564-1616 William Shakespeare

1564 Birth of Puritanism

1598 Edict of Nantes grants Huguenots religious freedom.

1611 Authorized King James Version of the Bible produced.

1618 Synod of Dort refutes Arminianism in favor of Calvinism.

1614-1691 Brother Lawrence, author of The Practice of the Presence of God.

1620 Pilgrims land at Plymouth.

1628-1688 John Bunyan, author of The Pilgrim's Progress.

1636 Puritans found Harvard.

1642-1727 Isaac Newton discovers color in light; laws of gravity, motion.

1647-1748 Isaac Watts writes over 700 hymns and 25 books.

1648 Westminster Confession of Faith. Reformed doctrines of the Church clarified.

1648-1717 Madame Guyon, pens Experiencing Union with God Through Inner Prayer.

1651-1715 Francois Fenelon, author of Maxims of the Saints, Spiritual Letters and Christian Counsel.

1662 The Act of Conformity forces over 2,000 Puritan pastors out of the Church of England.

1662-1714 Matthew Henry, author of Commentary on the Whole Bible

1667 John Milton publishes Paradise Lost.